SHOW TIME!

A Guide to Making Effective Presentations

ELIZABETH P. TIERNEY

Oak Tree Press
Dublin

This book was typeset by
Seton Music Graphics, Ltd., Bantry, Co. Cork for
Oak Tree Press, 4 Arran Quay, Dublin 7

© 1994 Elizabeth P. Tierney

Illustrations and cover design by Aileen Caffrey
A catalogue record for this book
is available from the British Library

ISBN 1-872853-47-1

Printed in Ireland by
Colour Books, Ltd., Dublin

CONTENTS

Chapter 1

INTRODUCTION

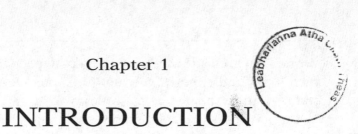

"I often tell the story of the first time I gave a speech. I was so nervous that I kept my eyes closed through most of the monologue. I kept hoping that if I didn't look at them they would quietly go away. When I had finished, I opened my eyes and discovered that, unfortunately, my wish had been granted. There was only one person left in the audience. He was a bookish-looking fellow wearing a sour expression. Hoping to find some solace in this catastrophe, I asked him why he stayed. Still frowning, he replied, ' I'm the next speaker.'"
—Victor Kiam, American Businessman

"I'll be OK."
"I'll be fine."
"It'll be over soon."

This may sound like the mutterings of a hospital patient who is being wheeled on a trolley to the operating theatre. Actually, they are the same reassurances that you might give yourself when you are introduced as the next speaker at a meeting, or when you enter a room, stare at the empty lectern and realise that you are next—it's show time!

Then, the medical analogy falls apart. In the operating theatre you lie on the table while skilled competent professionals work on you. If you are speaking, however, you are doing the work; you are not anaesthetised; you are not prone. You are wide awake and totally dependent on your own skills and competence, not on someone else's. Like the poor unfortunate on the trolley, you are worried. And being nervous is normal. Standing before an audience can be a scary experience. How scary? Well, the results of a survey conducted some years ago indicated that public speaking was perceived to be the second most frightening experience in your life. What was number one, you ask? Dying!

Why is making a presentation so terrifying? There are good reasons: you are alone, you are unprotected, you are vulnerable to attack, you are standing in front of other people who are sitting, who are looking at you and who

expect something from you—great things. No matter how much ego you have, you are convinced that you will make a fool of yourself, that you will risk looking bad in the eyes of your colleagues, friends, subordinates or superiors. The individuals in that audience are in a position to make judgements about you, and about what you know, and they will. Now, that is unnerving!

While you are trying to reassure yourself like the hospital patient and failing to do so, you are also undermining what confidence you may have by asking yourself questions like: Will I sound stupid? Will I get the job? The client? The referral? Will I be promoted? Relegated? Thanked? Ignored? Humiliated? Such a barrage of questions produces anxiety. But remember this is self-inflicted. You are doing it to yourself.

Making a presentation does not have to be so disquieting, daunting or terrifying. The ideas and recommendations that you will read in this book are written to help you realise that although worrying is normal, you can get past the fear. Effective presentation is not a gift from the gods to a select few. It is neither a mystery nor something you are taught at your mother's knee. Anyone can learn to speak well.

Presentation involves both a process and a product. Of course, having some innate talent does not hurt, but anyone with a basic understanding of some of the techniques involved in speaking will have a better understanding of how to hold an audience's attention. Being aware of these techniques will help develop your strengths and diminish your weaknesses as a speaker. In addition, anyone who understands and accepts some underlying principles and techniques about presenting will be a speaker who is more polished and confident. Anyone who accepts the importance of finding time to practice and to seek feedback will be more effective and self-aware. Anyone who develops the habit of asking some key preliminary questions will become a successful speaker, one whose ideas are considered, whose recommendations are weighed and who will earn the plaudits of the audience. In time, nervous but not terrified, you may welcome the opportunity to speak in public; you may even enjoy it.

By the end of this chapter, you will have read the underlying principles of making successful presentations; subsequent chapters will address the techniques, the need for practice and the key questions that you should ask before you speak. Although these principles are dealt with separately for analytical purposes, each one of them is an integral part of the whole act of talking to a group.

Specifically, each chapter focuses on an element of presentation, from a review of the communications process itself to the using of notes and the handling of visuals. But read no further if your purpose is to learn manipulation or demagoguery. These pages are designed to help you become a more comfortable, believable and effective speaker, not an unethical or deceitful one. Taken to an extreme, effective speaking and image management can hide and even distort the truth.

Let's articulate some more of those pre-speaking concerns, because getting them out in the open is healthy. If you recognise yourself in some of the worries, perhaps you may not be so lonely knowing that you are not the only one feeling so miserable. Do you really think that you are the only one who has endured these self-doubts? You are not. Even public figures, people accustomed to speaking, feel queasy when they face an audience.

So, what are you really worried about? Do you think you will sound stupid? Do you worry that the audience knows more about the subject than you do? Do you worry that you are going to bore those people to death? Do you

worry that you are going to forget what you had planned
to say? About going blank? Do you worry that the content
will be waffle? Any one of these nagging questions has the
potential to undermine your self-esteem, whether you are
in front of an audience at a dinner, a wedding, an interview, a class, or at a board, department or sales meeting.

Behind the reassurances and those nagging questions
lurks the real issue. You know in your heart that it is not
your talk that is being judged. You are. Somehow, you
think, your name, career or reputation is at stake. With all
that baggage, it is no wonder that surgery appears to be a
more pleasant option than speaking. With a general or
local anaesthesia, you could sleep through the proceedings,
or at least minimise the pain.

The degree of discomfort that speakers feel is revealed by their choice of words as they describe their feelings after they have given a talk. "I'm so relieved!" or "I survived." Notice, not "great!" or "excited". They are settling for survival. But what you need to do to succeed is to turn the experience around and focus on the positive implications of giving a talk rather than on the negative ones.

This book is written not only to assist you in being more at ease with the process and with yourself, but also because—forgive me, Michael Porter—being an effective presenter gives you a competitive advantage. You will interview better, run meetings better, talk to clients better, give after-dinner speeches better. Humans have not totally been replaced by technology yet. We still communicate face to face, individually and in groups, and the more comfortable and effective you are as a speaker, the more opportunities you create for yourself or for your organisation.

What is written here is based on years of experience coaching teachers, trainers, students and business men and women, as well as on my own experience as a speaker, trainer and lecturer. It is based on the mistakes I have made and on the lessons I have learned and continue to learn. For one, I will never forget that dark day when one of my own dreaded fears was realised. It was the day that I took one look at the lens of the camera in front of me and, despite my planning, remembered nothing. My mind was a complete blank.

On the other hand, I will also never forget the delightful occasion when I decided to take a lengthy pause during a speech and could sense the power as the audience waited for the next words. I have also learned from attending meetings and conferences and from watching speakers. I suspect I have learned the most, though, from watching the audience's response to the speakers that they are listening to. I watch individuals nod off, or stare out the window or glance at their watches. I have also watched the eager faces of the people who are enthralled by what they are hearing. To repeat, these pages are written with the conviction that you can learn to give an effective presentation, to be less nervous, to have greater impact on those who are listening to you and thus ultimately for your growth and self-esteem.

Let's begin by looking at the four principles that underlie all presentations. They are:

1. You have a responsibility to the audience.
2. You should make conscious decisions about what you are presenting and not rely on your intuition alone.
3. You should make decisions before, during and after you speak.
4. You should become aware of your own strengths and weaknesses as a presenter and practise using techniques that will enhance your talk.

Let's look at each one of these principles.

Be Responsible to the Audience

Frequently, speakers are so self-absorbed that they forget about the people in front of them. They often behave like primary school students who have been told to memorise a poem in order to recite it in class. Remember when recitation time came, each student got up and recited the poem as quickly as possible, eyes glued to the floor, oblivious to books falling, cars honking, doors slamming?

Have you ever heard or used the phrase, "Thanks for listening" at the end of a talk? Children do not say that; adults do. It is a revealing expression in that it suggests that the audience made the effort on your behalf, when, in fact, you are working on theirs. If you as a speaker do all that you need to do in preparation and accept the responsibility that you have to be interesting, challenging, articulate and/or entertaining, then you will not need to thank the audience for listening. They will listen, and they will thank you when it is over for the effort that you made for them. In other words, the responsibility you have to those people before you is to be clear, sensitive and analytical. You need to determine what will work for that unique group listening to you. Remember, too, that time is a valuable resource. The audience is giving up their time, has chosen not to do something else in order to hear what you have to say. Not to make you more nervous, but that puts the responsibility for the audience squarely on your shoulders.

Make Conscious Decisions

You should make conscious decisions about what you are doing when you speak and not rely on your intuition alone. In other words, do not rely solely on your gut instincts on the day to advise you what to do. To be effective, you should be thinking about every aspect of the talk—what you are wearing, where and how you are going to stand, how to use your voice and when to turn the overhead on or off.

For example, do you use acetates just because other speakers use acetates? Do you wear the blue tie because it is in the closet? Do you stand behind the table or lectern because there is one in the room? Are you being reactive or proactive? You should be asking yourself: Is the blue tie right for this particular occasion or is it too washed out or too strong? Are acetates necessary and, if so, what for and why? Should I stand behind the lectern or table? Or should

I have it removed because my proximity to the audience will make me look more remote or more involved? In other words, decide what you have to do to be effective on that occasion.

Make Decisions Before, During and After

This principle involves decision-making, too. You should make decisions before, during and after you speak. No, not just about the colour of the tie, the number of acetates or the use of the lectern. Many of the decisions are interdependent.

For example, if you know that you have 30 minutes to speak, then you have to choose what information to include and what to exclude to fit within the time frame. During your speech, suppose that several members of the audience are nodding off, and if according to principle one, you assume responsibility for them, then you know that you have to make changes. What these changes will be requires immediate decisions on your part: lowering your voice, raising it, cutting out part of your talk, pounding the table, doing something. Then, after the talk is over you need to think about your original planning as well as what you did during the speech. You need to reflect on what you may have forgotten to take into consideration initially and also analyse what worked. That way you incorporate what you learned into your decision-making for the next talk. On to principle number four.

Be Aware of Your Strengths and Weaknesses

You should be aware of your own strengths and weaknesses as a speaker and practise those techniques that will

enhance your presentation style. Most of us recognise that
dancers, poets, athletes, painters have talent. However, we
tend to forget that to develop that talent, they have acquired
and practised techniques that enhance their innate ability.
It is not sheer passion on the day that wins an Olympic
Gold, nor is it merely enthusiasm that enables an actor to
muster the energy for the 100th performance. Actors and
athletes cannot rely simply on being in the mood on the
day. They have a job to do; they have years of practice and
a wealth of techniques to sustain them. You, as a presenter,
need to understand, in the same way, that there are techniques that will enhance your skills in presentation. All
you need to do is assess your own strengths and weaknesses
and to incorporate those techniques. This book will help
to show you how.

In summary, it is normal to be nervous before making a
presentation, but there is no reason to be so terrified that
you hurt yourself personally and professionally. You start
by accepting the four principles that can make a difference in the quality of your presentation:

1. You have a responsibility to the audience.
2. You should make conscious decisions about what you
   are presenting and not rely on your intuition alone.
3. You should make decisions, before, during and after
   you speak.
4. You should become aware of your own strengths and
   weaknesses as a presenter and practise using techniques
   that will enhance your talk.

Understand and implement these principles and you are
on the way to success as a speaker.

Chapter 2

HOW WE COMMUNICATE

"How well we communicate is determined not by how well
we say things but by how well we are understood."
—Andrew S. Grove, CEO, Intel Corporation

"What we have here is a failure to communicate."
—from the movie *Cool Hand Luke*

Before examining in detail the techniques that will enhance
your own presentation style, let's step back and examine
from a theoretical perspective what happens when we communicate. Doing that should enable you to analyse a process that is both instantaneous and taken for granted. We
do not think about it. This chapter should serve to remind
you of exactly what you are doing when you speak and
then to highlight some of the difficulties that are inherent
in the process of trying to share ideas with each other.

Based on that increased awareness of the process, you
should then be in a better position to assess what you
can do as a speaker to minimise the difficulties and increase the odds of having your ideas understood and then
acted upon.

Basically, the two-way communications process requires
both a sender and a receiver. Some people compare it to a
tennis or ping-pong match. One author compared the
communications process to the disassembling of London
Bridge in England stone by stone and sending it across
the pond to be reassembled in Arizona.

The process begins when the sender has an idea or a feeling, which is called a message. That message may be as simple as "Hello" or as complex as a strategic business plan or architectural design. Regardless of its complexity or level of abstraction, it is a message which emanates from the sender and is intended for the receiver.

The next step in the process is the sender's responsibility as well. The idea or concept, the message, needs to be encoded before it is sent. There are choices of codes: words, pictures, possibly signals. For example, suppose you are the sender. You recognise a friend in a store. You want to greet her, so you decide to encode your message with a signal, a gesture. Having made that encoding decision, you now raise your hand and transmit the greeting by moving your upraised arm quickly from side to side—you wave. But your friend has moved into the next aisle and does not see you.

You try a different code: words, spoken words. The message remains the same, but this time you encode and transmit it in another way. The encoded message is: "Hello, Deirdre!" transmitted with words spoken aloud. Notice you chose to say, "Hello", not "Bonjour", you selected English, not French, when you decided to speak to her. But in the crowd you have missed Deirdre again. However, you do know her home phone number, so that evening you continue coding your message in English words. You phone her; she is not in, and you speak to her answering machine. This time you lengthen the message: "Hi Deirdre. Saw you at the store. Sorry I missed you. Please phone me at the office." Days pass, and there is no word from Deirdre. Unwilling to give up, you decide to send the message one more time encoded again in English, but this time in writing—a letter.

"D. Tried to say 'Hello' at the store, but missed you. Phoned on Monday, but you were out. Please give me a shout at the office."

The message, now longer, remains essentially "hello." You have continued to use English, but over time you have varied your transmission from non-verbal language, the wave, to the spoken word, both in the store and on the answering machine and finally the written word, your letter. Sad to say, despite your efforts, Deirdre still fails to respond. The critical next step in the communications process does not occur. The message is not received. There was a message, it was encoded in different ways and transmitted differently, too, but two-way communication cannot be achieved without that next step: the receipt of the message.

Good news. Deirdre finally rings you at work and begins her conversation with "I got your letter. Sorry that I did not see you at the store and missed your phone call." With those words of Deirdre's you are assured that she received the message, decoded it accurately and acted on it by doing as you asked: she phoned you.

Examined this way, communicating is a straightforward, simple process. Giving a talk, not saying "hello" to a friend in a store, involves the same steps: identifying the message, encoding it in an appropriate language, then transmitting it so that the audience in front of you receives your ideas, decodes them, acts or does not act on them and then gives you feedback. Simple. No problem, you say.

Sorry. Problems. Lots of them. To be an effective speaker you need to be sensitive to the blockages in communication, because any one of them can have significant implications for your success in having your ideas received and/or acted upon. Let's look at some problems, starting as we did earlier with the initial message.

Have a Clear Message

Obviously, any topic that you plan to talk about is going to be far more sophisticated and complicated than "hello."

Whatever the topic is, you must think the message through carefully. Even if you encode it precisely and transmit it thoughtfully, without a clear initial message your ideas may be confused. Back to London Bridge: it was dismantled, sent, received and reassembled, but the purchaser thought he was buying the Tower Bridge. The message was confused. You have experienced the problem. You have probably walked out of a room after someone else's talk saying "What was that about?" or "Well, that was a waste of a morning!" or "What was the point of that?!" That is feedback and it suggests that the message itself was either unclear or not worthwhile to the listener. So you need to think through your purpose. Chapter 7 is designed to help you refine your thinking about the intent of your talk.

Select Your Words Carefully

Let's assume, however, that you have worked out a clear message. Perhaps you need to explain the implications of a new centralised recruiting system. Sounds good. Now let's look at some encoding problems. Earlier, you decided against sending a message to Deirdre in French. In that situation, that decision may have been an easy one. You knew that Deirdre speaks only English, but if you do not spend time thinking about the implications of your code choice, you can easily select an inappropriate one. To make a point, in the extreme, you would most likely not translate your talk on the centralised recruiting system into Latin and then intone it to the audience in a Gregorian chant, just as an architect would not write building plans for a contractor in iambic pentameter. Annual reports are not collections of family snapshots, nor does the ground staff at Shannon Airport prepare a fax for a pilot to indicate where the plane should be parked.

As silly as these examples are, inadvertently you can make a silly encoding decision, too. For example, if you decide to encode your talk in a specialised language that is technical or germane only to specialists in fields that have their own vocabulary, such as medicine, insurance, law or information technology, those members of the audience who are unfamiliar with that language will be unable to decipher what your message is. There would be a similar problem if you chose to speak Dutch to an all French-speaking audience. In essence, you need to think hard about the choice of code.

It is not just foreign languages or technical language that can be problematic. The audience may be unable to decode what you are saying, if your talk is filled with jargon. Are you throughputting, inputting; vertically challenging, synergising, or moving goal posts? Like the contractor unable to visualise the building, or the pilot waiting in vain to park the aircraft, your audience may not be able to act on what you say if they cannot decipher your meaning because of the use of clichés or jargon that are alien to them.

Meaning itself constitutes another problem. "I thought you said two," remarked Tom.

"No, I meant 'also', not 'two'," said Bill.

If an American walks into a shop in Ireland and is asked if he or she is OK, it is possible that he will wonder if he is looking ill. "Are you OK?" is English, but it means something other than "May I help you?" in a non-Irish culture. There was a famous comedy routine about the man who got a traffic ticket for making a U turn in a one way street. He understood "NO U TURN" to mean "No; you turn."

Therefore, as a speaker you not only need to be concerned about the clarity of your initial message, but you also have to take time to be sensitive to your choice of code, if you want your message received as it was intended. Again, let's suppose that the message is meaningful, the code choice appropriate. What else can go wrong?

Understand Transmission Problems

Getting the message to the receiver can be another problem. Remember Deirdre? Perhaps the store was crowded and noisy, so she did not hear you when you spoke, nor did she see you when you waved. You did phone her, and although you did leave a message on her answering machine, her phone might have been busy when you called or a radio on when the phone was answered or even static on the line. Our poor pilot may finally get the fax about where to park, but perhaps only the left side of it will be received, the right is blurred.

As a speaker, you will not have to worry about answering machines or blurred faxes, but you will have to be ready to address issues like noise, disruptions, acoustics problems, microphones that do not work, the clarity of your speech pattern, your ability to project your voice in a large room, or the quality and choice of your visuals. Anticipating and handling these problems is up to you. Remember, you have the responsibility. You are the sender. You have control of the first three steps in the communications process: the message, the choice of code and its transmission.

Know Your Audience

Once you have transmitted that message, you lose control of it; it moves to the receiver and therein lie more problems for you as a speaker. Suppose the receivers do not like you. It will not make any difference what pains you take to prepare, receivers may interpret your message in terms of their perceptions of you. "There he goes, profiling again!" "Just trying to show the rest of us up." Suppose it is not your personality but your values that are annoying to the receivers. You may have a view on religion, on abortion, on homosexuality or on Manchester United, for that matter, that the receivers find repugnant or offensive. So your message may be rejected even if the subject of your talk has nothing to do with those issues.

But then you may not be the problem, the receiver may be. Deirdre may not have heard you in the store, not because she was out of earshot, but because she was preoccupied, concerned with the time, and she wanted to leave the store before the traffic became too heavy. In the same way, someone in your audience could be preoccupied with a personal problem like a large payment due on a credit card bill or a deadline for a report that is fast approaching, or an excessively absent staff member who needs to be counselled. In other words, the receiver may like you, but may be distracted by non-work or work-related issues.

Let's complicate the speaking business still more. It is important to remember that the receiver, your audience, can process information more quickly than you can speak it, which means that no matter how interesting or relevant the subject matter is, the receiver has the capability of listening to you and thinking about other issues at the same time: planning holidays, thinking about lunch, picking up a video, anticipating an afternoon meeting, scheduling a phone call. That ability mentally to handle more information than you can provide while speaking is a problem for you. No, the solution is not to speak faster to fill up the space—it is to keeping their attention by being interesting.

Earlier there was a reference to the quality of your visuals. Let's not focus on the spoken word to the exclusion of the visual. Remember that pictures send messages and that most speakers choose to add some kind of visuals to their talks. You have undoubtedly experienced most of the encoding and transmission problems caused by visuals, because you have seen them when you were a member of an audience: the print that is too small, the graph without the label, the chart with too many trends, the slide with too many words, the acetate that is too big for the screen, the picture that is blurred, distorted or reversed—concerns, issues, worries. Maybe you have a cause to be nervous!

By breaking a complex process into simpler components, and by highlighting some of the difficulties that may occur by looking at the problems of sending a simple greeting to a friend, you can become more sensitive to the importance of making conscious decisions about the message, the code and the means of transmission in advance of any lengthy talk you give. You also can see how important it is to know your receivers, and why it is unwise to be overly dependent on your instincts. Communication breaks down. If you are aware of potential problems, then you can plan and organise for them. That attention to detail is one of the hallmarks of a good speaker.

So, by looking at the theoretical communications model you can begin to appreciate:

- The need to have a clear message when you speak.
- The need to select your words, pictures and gestures thoughtfully.
- The need to transmit what you have to say clearly.
- The need to know your audience.

Consequently, the receiver/audience, will understand the implications of that new centralised recruitment policy so clearly that you will not have 12 phone messages on your desk after your talk asking you questions about that new policy, questions already answered in your speech. Nor will you have to write three additional memos clarifying what you already said in your talk the previous day.

By having a clearer understanding of what is involved in the two-way communications process, the mystery about speaking fades, your responsibility becomes clearer and your confidence should increase because you will know what to do.

So far, our focus has been on verbal language and with a brief reference to the language of images, let's focus on non-verbal language as an important means of communication. It is a key element for you as a speaker, because while the audience is listening to your words and looking at the slides, you and what you are *doing* are the focus of their attention.

Chapter 3

NON-VERBAL LANGUAGE

"We all, in one way or another, send our little messages to the world . . . and rarely do we send our messages consciously. We act out our state of being with nonverbal body language. We lift one eyebrow for relief. We rub our noses for puzzlement. We clasp our arms to isolate ourselves or to protect ourselves. . . . The gestures are numerous, and while some are deliberate . . . there are some that are mostly unconscious."
—Julius Fast, author of *Body Language*

This chapter examines two main themes: (1) how the way you use your body when you are speaking and what you are wearing can enhance your ability to get your message across, and (2) how, conversely, your body and clothing can become yet another problem in the litany of barriers that may interfere with your audience's ability to receive, decode and act on the ideas that you have laboured over for days or weeks in preparation for your talk.

To increase your awareness of the importance of non-verbal language on your audience the first step is to recognise the messages that certain types of body language can send to an audience and thus affect your presentation. You may begin to identify some of your own habits. So, pat yourself on the back for your good ones and begin to work on eliminating those gestures or actions that take away from your performance—one at a time. Pick one aspect to work on at a time, then another. You will only feel frustrated if you tackle it all at once. Every diet book tells you to focus on the success of losing one pound at a time not on the fact that you have ten to go before you reach your desired weight.

Let's begin to look at some of the specific physical aspects of presentation—what the audience sees: your head, your face, your arms and hands, your gestures and stance, your legs and your feet. Let's look at each of these to see how your use of them can interfere with your audience's ability to concentrate on your words and at the same time to see what you might do to reinforce the verbal message by sending appropriate non-verbal messages. Simply put, your choice or control of the physical aspects of presentation should reinforce your message, not interfere with it. An extreme example is the habit of speaking with one hand over your mouth. Obviously, you risk not being understood or heard. But some speakers actually do that, and are not aware of the habit. Along the way, you may notice some of your own idiosyncrasies, both positive and negative.

Please, do not beat yourself up if you recognise five or six negatives. This is not a contest. To repeat, pick one and try to change that one. Then, after you have made headway, pick another one and work on it. Athletes like Linford Christie or Stephen Roche did not master all the techniques required in their respective fields in one day or one week. It takes time, effort, patience and a pat on the back. And there is nothing wrong with giving yourself that pat on the back!

Your Head and Face

So, let's begin at the top of your body and work down. Heads move up and down or side to side. If, as you speak, you let your head wobble, you may look like a large, featherless bird. Suppose you deliver your entire talk with your head tilted to one side; you may appear to the audience to be demure or coquettish wistfully begging for their support or sympathy. If your talk is about the implications of down-sizing—a serious subject—and through the entire speech you have your head tilted to one side, with your shoulder raised to meet it, you will probably look coy or kittenish, not exactly the look for a captain of industry. If you hold your head up with your chin aloft, on the other hand, you may risk looking smug or arrogant.

Imagine, too, shaking your head from side to side to signify what we in Ireland recognise as the signal for "no", and yet your words are saying "yes", how "delighted" you are to be here speaking on this occasion. Or the reverse may be true: you are shaking your head, up and down to signal "yes," when you are saying that "there is definitely no problem with our emissions." In other words, unless you take care, your head may be sending one message, while your words are sending another, a mixed message:

"yes" with your words, but "no" with your head, or "yes" with your words and "no" with your head. The way you hold your head can also make you appear shy or smug when all you wanted was to appear straightforward.

Facial expressions, too, may be a problem. It's remarkable how speakers allow their faces to become grim when they speak to an audience no matter what the subject. Not all talks in business are eulogies. As a matter of fact, even a eulogy can include some happy remembrances. In other words, your facial expression should reinforce your message. You are worried, but let your face light up, try smiling or looking happy. When you say "Good morning" or "Good afternoon", a look of genuine pleasure is warranted, even if you are nervous. If you are "pleased with the outcome of the study," if you are "delighted with the recommendations," if you are "excited at the prospect," then, for heaven's sake, look pleased or delighted or excited. That does not mean that you wear a grin from ear to ear for the duration of the talk, nor should you grin if you are saying that you are "concerned" with the findings, "worried" about the non-compliance, "disturbed" by the competition. Once again your face should mirror your words. Because you are likely to be nervous, you will probably have no difficulty looking worried. It is much harder to smile. But it also helps you feel better. Try it. The warmth that you emit has an impact on the audience. Remember how you felt when you walked into your classes years ago. In one room you were greeted by a smiling teacher and in another by a tight-lipped snarler. Know that you can produce the same feelings in an audience. You can affect their level of interest or motivation by exuding a feeling of warmth or by looking cold and distant. Smiles work wonders. In retrospect, the classes I dreaded were taught by cold, distant and stern teachers.

Your Eyes

Now that you are holding your head up and trying to smile, sometimes, what about those eyes of yours? Yes, everyone knows that we should make eye contact. Do you really understand why? Do you genuinely look at people and, more important, do you see what you are looking at? Really see? You should be looking at every face in the audience, not talking over their heads, or out of the window, or intoning into the upper left hand corner of the room.

Because by looking at each face you are signalling to the audience that you like them, that you have nothing to hide, that you are honest, open and direct. And by looking *and* seeing those faces and reactions, you are also able to get immediate feedback, a critical dimension in the two-way communication process—unlike Deirdre who didn't give us feedback until she finally returned the phone call.

In Chapter 4 you will learn what to do with what you see. For the moment let's stay with the looking. When you look at everyone, do not start at the left side of the room and move your eyes methodically to the right, or start at the right to move then to the left like a periscope in search of a target.

Look at everyone randomly. And "everyone" means just that, not only the person whom you perceive to be the power figure in the room—the one with the title. Even Don Corleone had a consigliere. In other words, be careful not to assume that all decisions are made unilaterally by the MD, the President, the Chair, the Department Head. People in power seek advice from different people and those people may be there, too.

Another good reason for looking at faces is that when you look at someone that person will usually return the glance. Thus, people pay attention. In addition, you are sending the message with your eyes that you value every-one in the room. Everyone is important. Please do not have staring contests; a few seconds on a face is enough. One caveat, though: watch out for the "nodder". There is always someone in the room who is hanging on your every word and nodding in agreement with every word you say—a friend. Thank goodness! But do not be misled. You are nervous, so you are grateful for some reassurance. As a speaker, when you are feeling vulnerable, it is easy to lock your eyes onto that nodding head like a guided missile. Soon you will find that you are directing your talk only at that individual to the neglect of the others in the room. While you may have successfully developed a rela-tionship with one person, the others may stop listening and may even resent your neglect. The audience may have similar feelings if you speak predominantly to one side of the room. Catch yourself if you do, and work to correct that fault so that you involve everyone.

Your Body

But now, what about those appendages that are connected to your shoulders—your arms? And those additional bits at the end—your hands? What a nuisance they are for a speaker! Where did they come from, you ask, and worse yet, what do you do with them? Just as you have seen poor visuals, you have also witnessed all the attempts by speakers to solve the arm-hand problem. Can you remem-ber them?

- The speakers with their arms glued to their sides; they look like trees or totem poles.
- The speakers who rid themselves of the darn things by clasping them behind their backs.

- The speakers who wish to appear nonchalant and seek to do so by putting one hand in a pocket or sometimes one hand in each pocket. Sometimes the speaker forgets and begins to play with the 57p in his pocket— another noisy distraction.
- The speakers who take a more defensive posture: crossing their arms across their chests—a variation is crossing the arms with the hands held together as if in prayer. Not only does the speaker appear to be fending off attack, but with the added hand gesture seeks divine intervention as well. While some seek to protect the vulnerable upper body, others, perhaps because of a healthy knowledge of the perils of soccer, protect themselves lower down.

None of these solutions is ideal. What happens is that instead of looking open and confident, you are signalling to the audience that you are either stiff, insecure, scared, or defensive. The truth is that you may feel that way, but do not shout it at your audience with a non-verbal message when you want your verbal message to sound strong, open and honest.

So, what do you do? First of all, remember that non-verbal language should reinforce your verbal message, not contradict or undermine it. In effect, you are a living visual. Your head, hands and arms can all be used to assist you in communicating your ideas. Although it takes practice to unglue that arm from your side, or take one hand out of a pocket, learn to use them and move them just the way that you do when you are having a conversation with someone.

To become more self-aware, have a chat with a friend, and watch how both of you use your hands as you talk to make a point or to make a gesture. Notice how useful

your fingers are for counting or for making points: "The three advantages of . . .", "Two reasons why . . .". But in speaking be careful not to script your movements. By that is meant deciding in advance to touch your chest every time you use the word, "I", or pointing to the audience every time you say "you". You will begin to look like a marionette. Try to talk conversationally and use your hands naturally. For example, if something you are describing is large, show how large with your hand; if it is heavy, heft it. How do people describe the size of the salmon they caught? With their hands. Do be careful, though, of wringing your hands, particularly when the subject of your talk is financial. Rather than appearing to be a business person, you may look like Fagin. And avoid pointing at the audience under any circumstance, with your finger, with a pen, with a pointer. It is a threatening gesture and may offend them. Try to use an open, whole hand, not just your index finger poking at your audience as if you were prodding the bad guy's chest or aiming a gun at him.

Again, use your entire body to reinforce your message, to emphasise your points, not to confuse or distract your audience. That point is equally true of your legs, your feet and your stance. Unless you are an actor in a grade B cowboy movie, try to keep both hips even, not one up and one down.

When you walk up to the front of the platform, stand with assurance. Plant each foot in a line directly below each of your shoulders to support your weight evenly. If you press both feet together, you may appear to be on the verge of toppling over, and your audience might very well be waiting for you to do just that. Do you take dance positions with your feet or actually begin to dance the tango or cha-cha? Some speakers rock from side to side or roll up and down on their toes. Don't. Still others cross their ankles while they are standing or bend their ankles as if they were just learning to ice skate. Remember you want to appear strong, open and confident, not like the leaning tower of Pisa or an extra in an early Clint Eastwood western, with your hips and shoulders akimbo, hands in the pocket.

And don't be afraid to move. You should feel free to walk normally, confidently, not in mincing steps like Mr Bean or like a caged animal pacing in a tight space, but move. Speak from the right, move to the left, if it is appropriate or warranted. There are no rules against moving so long as you do so with clear purpose. Movement creates interest and energises your talk.

By the way, there are added benefits to standing up straight, chest up, shoulders relaxed. Your voice will be stronger and you will be able to maintain eye contact better. It is easy to lean on furniture, to welcome any kind of support, even if it is from a wooden dais. But if you do, you will look tired or lazy, casual or frightened to your audience, so try to avoid holding on to desks or lecterns or leaning against furniture. By the way, a big man with a big voice, leaning in toward the audience can appear threatening. Stand tall and look open. Your heart may be pounding, but you will look and sound self-assured.

There is one additional category of non-verbal messages: idiosyncratic gestures. You need to discover whether you have any particular gestures that are distracting, like repeatedly putting that stray length of hair behind your ear, or frequently tossing your head to get the fringe out of your eyes or pushing your glasses up onto your nose, or scratching your head, or pulling your ear. There is nothing wrong with any of these gestures. You are human, after all, and they are normal, but when any are repeated so often that the audience begins to notice them they are a problem. What happens is that your listeners begin to pay more attention to the frequency with which you straighten your tie, or fix your hair, or push your glasses up on your nose than to your calculations about your company's market share.

Your Clothing

Since a tie was mentioned earlier, it is time to talk about your choice of clothing. If you think of presenting in terms of the theatre world, then consider your clothes as your costume. They need to be selected with care. They should match the occasion. All of you, the whole package, is under scrutiny: what you say, how you use your body and what you are wearing. No, it is not that the audience will notice brown buttons or black ones, but they will notice unpolished shoes. Gentlemen beware: they will notice the holes in your socks; ladies, take care: are there ladders in your tights? You risk the audience thinking that if you are sloppy about those details, perhaps you will be sloppy about the ideas that you are discussing as well. I remember seeing a speaker wearing an overcoat during a talk. It was a cold room, but we wondered whether she was in a hurry to leave.

In addition to wearing something appropriate, choose something comfortable. No, not jeans and trainers. Because of the responsibility that you have and the amount you have on your mind, select clothing that is going to be problem-free: no tight collars, no shoes that pinch, no buttons that open, no scarves that slide off, no skirts that ride up.

And, the day that you present is the day to wear the suit or jacket that looks best on you and that fits you well. Pass up the trouser with the cuffs bunching around your ankles, or the jacket in which your hands are lost up your sleeves. You do not want to look like you are wearing a basketball player's uniform. For men, be sure, too, that the collar of the shirt closes and fits you at the neck. Lost any buttons? Replace them. Select a tie that remains knotted and that will stay comfortably at the neck to cover that collar button. Before you get up to speak, straighten that tie and do it just once. Just like fixing your hair or playing with your glasses, repeated tie fixing is a distraction. Forgive the familiarity, but are your trousers around your waist? Or are you hiking them up regularly? Perhaps braces or a tighter belt is in order.

What colours to select? What styles to wear? Those are your decisions to make, too. You know what makes you look good. There are books on the subject of colour and style for your skin tones and build. There are certain fashions and colours that look better on some people. Decide whether a double-breasted suit is the most flattering for your height and weight. Why select an outfit that is in fashion, but that makes you look shorter or heavier than you are? If you are not built for the latest design, go for a classic look and hold out for the style to change. If purple is this year's colour, but it is not yours, select the colour that looks good on you. Pale yellow or green makes me look as though a trip to the doctor's surgery is in order. High contrast like black against white or navy against white gives you an image of higher authority. Charcoal grey against a light background is another. Think about where you have seen those colour combinations worn. Blue against yellow or beige against yellow are softer, friendlier combinations. Maybe you should consider wearing brighter colours on drearier days. For the talk on Tuesday after the bank holiday, or on a Monday morning? In other words, your choice of clothing is another important decision.

Finding the right "costume" may be harder for women than for men, who usually do not have to make as many choices about what to wear. Your decision should be governed by the words, "appropriate for the occasion": long skirt, short skirt, slacks, pant suit, slit skirt and so on. The fuchsia mohair sweater, the see-through blouse with the décolletage, the three-inch earrings, or the skirt "for standing only" may not be right for the day. Each item in and of itself may be stunning on you, but if you are delivering a serious message that has implications for the organisation you represent, you need to ensure that the audience is focused on your face, your words, your overheads, your message, not on how stunning you are or what a great figure you have. No, you do not need to wear a three-piece suit. No, you do not have to dress like a man. If you err, do so on the conservative side. And wear comfortable shoes.

You look good. You have selected comfortable, appropriate clothes that do not distract. Make one more decision: how you wear your hair on the day. Is your hair in your eyes? Is the fringe too long? I have seen both men and women who appear to have only one eye or are fighting that independent strand of hair that keeps falling out of place.

And wear a watch. Check it from time to time to see that you are on schedule; you may need to speed up or slow down.

There is much to think about when you speak. You need to remember that you are sending non-verbal messages along with your verbal ones, so you should think about how you use your body, your head, your face, your arms and hands, the way you stand and move and then how you choose to dress on the day. There are no absolutes, no rules, but remember that you are making conscious decisions all the time, not leaving it all up to chance. You may decide that you are deliberately not going to smile, or that you want to take off your jacket and roll up your sleeves, or that you will sit on the table, or wear the tie that looks like a fish or the tights with sequins at the ankles. If you do, presumably you have decided that doing any or all of these things will have the impact that you want to have on your audience and that it will ultimately send them on their way remembering your message.

Chapter 4

VOICE AND SPEECH PATTERNS

"Proper words in proper places, make the true definition
of a style."
—Jonathan Swift

By now you are probably wondering how you are ever going to remember all this advice—look pleasant, but not all of the time; look at people's faces, but not for too long; use your hands to emphasise points, but not too often; stand tall and walk around, but do not pace. You haven't even begun to organise the talk yet. Before you can do the drafting, however, it is important to examine two more physical aspects of presentation: your voice and speech pattern and the impact they can have on your audience.

Many speakers take their voices for granted; in fact, by not taking advantage of what their voices can do, they undervalue them. You could take speech or elocution lessons, but there is much that you can do to improve the use of your voice and to modify your speech on your own. As always, the first step in the process involves awareness, recognising what you can do with your voice and speech pattern to take advantage of their potential for turning an OK talk into an excellent one.

Pacing

Let's begin with the speed at which you talk, the pace. If you learn to accelerate and decelerate, you are well on your way to improvement, because pacing is, in fact, one of the biggest stumbling blocks for the less seasoned presenter. There is good reason for this. Most people tend to speak too quickly when they stand up to talk in front of a group. Why? In part because they speak more quickly when they are nervous and they want to get the ordeal over with as quickly as possible. They rush. Remember the responsibility that you have to that audience. They need to be able to comprehend what you are saying. They are not in a position to engage you in conversation, to say "Would you mind clarifying that last point?" or "Did I understand you to mean . . .?" They are dependent on what you say and how you say it, so you need to speak slowly enough for them to capture the meaning without their being able to ask you questions throughout the talk.

Therefore, because you are more nervous at the beginning of a talk than at the end of it, overcompensate for that nervousness by speaking your opening sentences

slowly, ensuring that your first words do not all run together. Have you ever heard someone open with "Goodmorning-itisnicetoseeyou"? If that sounds like what it looks like, it will be hard to understand, and those people facing you will concentrate for a bit, but then may give up trying to follow you after awhile. Their eyes will glaze over and they will think of other things.

Pausing

You can always stop. Frequently, in their eagerness to be done, speakers race through the entire talk like the Dublin to Cork Express. Try to take a more leisurely route, make some local stops. Speed up through less important material, slow down through the nuts and bolts. And pause. Pick your moments, of course. Pausing is an excellent technique because it gives the audience a chance to take in your words, to absorb them. For example, speakers frequently build rhetorical questions into their talks: "Why should you buy widgets?" But then they do not give the audience time to think either about the question or about an answer. Suppose the speaker has decided to startle the audience with a new concept to implement within the organisation, for the sake of argument, the introduction of flex-time scheduling. Rather than making the recommendation for the scheduling and then pausing to permit the audience to get their heads around the idea, the speaker charges right into four justifications and six implications for the recommendation—each one of which may require some thought. While you are on point number nine, the audience may still be thinking about the original notion—flex-time. In addition, if you want the audience to have time to jot down some notes or questions as you speak, they will not be able to write anything if you are already talking

about justification number four, and they are still proces-
sing numbers two and three. So take appropriate pauses.

To repeat: slow down, particularly at the beginning, but
also throughout the talk when you are making key points.
Consider varying the pace, sometimes slow, sometimes
fast and sometimes pausing or stopping altogether, not just
for the sake of pausing or stopping, but because doing so
alters the impact of your talk and allows the audience time
to reflect. It also makes the talk more interesting to listen to,
thus helping to eliminate that concern about being boring.

Accents

Pacing has another implication, too. Suppose you come
from another part of the city, the country or the world than
where you are speaking—born in Athlone, speaking in
Detroit. You may have an accent that is unfamiliar to the
audience. If they are unused to certain sounds, they may
have difficulty decoding at first, so, once again, take your
time. Give the audience a chance to adjust to the way you
pronounce certain sounds. They will, in time. People who
have heavy regional accents are often advised to rid
themselves of them. If you have one but are understood
by others, don't change. Audiences welcome the difference.
If, however, you learn that there is a particular sound that
you make that may confuse or change the meaning of
what you are saying, then work on that single sound.
Avoid puzzling your audience as to whether you said
"three" or "tree".

Pitch

You are also more interesting to listen to if you vary the
pitch of your voice. The word "monotone" means just

that—one sound. Your voice, like a musical instrument, has a range. So by learning to raise or lower the pitch, you can avoid that "poor Johnny—one-note" quality. We do not speak all the time as a basso, an alto or a soprano. The very fact that in English our voices go up at the end of a sentence to signal to the listener that we are asking a question indicates that we are capable of varying the pitch. Don't you agree? Say that last sentence out loud and notice the number of pitch varieties possible. So, alter the pitch as you speak; it avoids that droning quality we have all heard and dread.

Volume

In addition to pacing and pitch, let's add volume to our list of variables. Notice how you are beginning to sound like a CD player? You know that you are capable of speaking

softly or loudly as well as somewhere in between, because
on the one hand, you have all whispered to a friend sitting
next to you at the cinema, and on the other, you have also
shouted with pleasure or dismay during a match. You can
raise and lower the volume. So add that ability to the rest
of your repertoire of talents. The options for creating verbal diversity, you will note, are increasing. "But I usually
speak softly," you say. Just slow down and stand tall, look
out, breathe deeply and project your voice to the back of
the room, not down at the table in front of you or, like the
primary school poem reciter, to the floor. You will be heard.

Projecting

In the previous chapter, maintaining eye contact was
mentioned as an important skill to develop. There was a
reference to both looking and to seeing. What follows is
an example of the importance of seeing what your audience
is doing and why presentation needs to be viewed as a
whole. Have you ever heard a speaker ask the question,
"Can you hear me in the back?" Why do speakers ask it?
Courtesy? It is a silly question. But the problem it raises is
a serious one: how can you be sure that those in the back
of the room can hear you?

If you are giving your talk in a large room and you are
worried about not being heard, one technique is to
imagine that your granny is seated in the back row, that
her hearing is not what it was, and that she is not wearing
a hearing aid. Project your voice to the back and direct
your opening remarks to her and to the people on either
side of her in the back row. When you speak your first
sentences, look at those people and see their reactions.
You will quickly discover whether they can hear you or
not. How do you know? Watch their non-verbal language.

They will send a message back to you. They may lean toward you or turn their heads so that their ears are directed toward you, suggesting that they are straining to hear, or the looks on their faces will show their reactions to your spoken words, thus indicating that they can hear you. There is no need to ask "Can you hear me in the back?" You can read the reaction without asking. And what would their usual answer be in any case? "No" means that they heard you ask the question, and "yes" means that they heard you as well. All the speaker has succeeded in doing by asking the question, therefore, is in disrupting the flow of the talk, particularly at that critical starting point. But then again, asking "Can you hear me in the back?" may be a great opening if "Hearing and Listening" is your topic for the day's talk.

So, in the early stages of your talk, in addition to making a conscious effort to adjust your volume, pace and pitch, project your voice to your granny in the back.

Extraneous Noises

Some of us make unnecessary sounds when we speak. To discover if you do, you may want to seek the help of a friend or borrow a cassette player or tape recorder. Speak to your friend or into the tape on any subject for a few minutes. When you play the tape back, or when your friend gives you feedback, what you are listening for are extraneous noises that you may be making when you talk. For example, you may not realise that you have the habit of saying "em" or "er" between words when you pause. You may make "tsk" or clicking sounds like some African singers because of the way you press your tongue against the roof of your mouth. You may smack your lips. No, it is not the end of the world if you do make any or all of those sounds, but like the other physical aspects of presentation, too many "em"s or "tsk"s may be distracting. What do you do to stop? First, become aware of the habit, then catch yourself in the act and try to avoid it the next time you do it. You will, though not every time. Slowly and steadily the noises will disappear, and you will replace the old habit with a new one—silence between words.

Besides making "tsk" and "em", some speakers actually "sigh" when they talk. That expulsion of a deep breath sounds sad or pitiful. "Poor me," it says. It does little to assist you in exciting that audience about a new concept or challenging project. Again, how do you stop? Just catch yourself. Remember that the first step in ridding yourself of these little mannerisms is awareness.

Clarity

If you use a cassette player, listen, too, for clarity in your speech pattern. Do your words have endings? Can you hear the final letters, the "s", "ing", the "d", the "t"? If you cannot hear them, you may be slurring your words which may cause the audience difficulty in deciphering. Does it sound like "GoomorninisnicetobespeakininAshfortoday?" Slow down and practise saying the ends of your words. There are also exercises you can use like repeating "she sells seashells by the seashore" or finding lines from poems or plays that you can practise: "Friend<u>s</u>, Roman<u>s</u>, Countrymen, len<u>d</u> me your ear<u>s</u>."

Emphasis

There is another point that should be made now. It is not related to pitch, pace, volume or clarity—it is emphasis.

For example, read each of the following sentences, empha-
sising the part of the sentence that is highlighted:

> *I* am delighted to be here today.
> I *am* delighted to be here today.
> I am *delighted* to be here today.
> I am delighted to be *here* today.
> I am delighted to be here *today*.
> *I am delighted* / to be here today.
> I am delighted / *to be here today*.

Remarkable, isn't it? By changing the emphasis, you can
change the meaning of the sentence. Think about this
when you are practising your talk. Decide whether there
are key phrases or words that will enhance your meaning
if you literally underline them with your voice. Please do
not over-rehearse. You'll begin to sound like a Stepford
Wife, not a human being. Remember this is about making
decisions—before, *during* and after, not all in advance.

In other words, when you are sending your message to
the audience what you do with your voice and speech will
assist you in assuring that your talk is both heard and
interesting. You have a number of variables to play with:
Pacing, Pausing, Pitch, Volume. And you may want to
think about your accent, your emphasis, your ability to
project and whether there are sounds that distract and
take away from your work.

Chapter 5

GETTING READY

"I keep six honest serving men
They taught me all I knew:
Their names are What and Why and When
And How and Where and Who."
—Rudyard Kipling

You have been reminded of what is involved in the two-way communication process and its problems. You are also becoming more aware of the implications of the physical aspects of presenting. Now it is time to look at the questions that you need to ask once you have been selected to speak or intend to speak. Getting the answers to them can increase your professional image as well as your confidence, because you will be more in control. You will encounter fewer surprises. In addition, some of the answers to these questions will help you make some necessary decisions in advance about how and what you are going to say.

What are these questions? No surprise. They are the five 'w's: who, what, where, why, when, plus five more: how, how many, how long, who else, and why me? Although we will look at each one individually, every question is, in fact, one more thread that will form the tapestry of your talk. Let's examine each question to understand, first, what you want to learn by asking it, and second, what implications the answers have for your decision-making.

42

"Why me?"

This is the last question on the list but we will deal with it first. It may sound silly, but this question is important because it seeks to determine why you and not someone else was selected to speak on this occasion. More often than not, the answer to the question should build your confidence, and thus assist in settling your nerves. More than likely the answer will be that "you are the best person to do it," or because "you have been closest to the project," which suggests that you "know your stuff," or you will be told that "you are good at presenting," which is also nice to hear. If, in the worst case scenario, you are told, "no one else wants to do it," you can still pat yourself on the back because the selector believes that you have the ability to give the talk. Thus, the answer to "why me?" should replace some of the negative self-doubts with more positive notions about your competence.

"How long?"

What you want to know is how much time should the talk take, including or in addition to any question time. The answer to the question will tell you if it is to be 10 minutes, 15 minutes or 25 minutes. Pin it down. Is it 15 minutes, plus 10 minutes for questions, a total of 25? Or is it 5 minutes with 10 minutes of questioning, a total of 15? Or is it 15 minutes with no questions? The answer may be that no one has thought about it yet. Press the issue and make a decision. The length of time you have has critical implications for what you select for the content. Whether you have 15 or 25 minutes to talk about new product development will mean that the degree of detail will vary enormously. Then again, are you going to talk at the audience for 25 minutes or will you need to involve them in some way?

The business of time is important. The amount of time you have to speak amounts to a contract with the audience. When you ask, "how long?", you must honour the answer. Ten minutes is 10 minutes, not 15. Twenty-five minutes is not 35 minutes. Have you ever had a 10.30 appointment somewhere, and been kept waiting until 11.00? Everyone responsible for that delay was, I am sure, apologetic, but how did you feel? Annoyed? Angry? Impatient? Frustrated? Kicking yourself for being on time? Thinking about what else you might be doing besides reading old copies of *HELLO!* or *Business and Finance*? You elicit exactly the same feelings in others when you speak longer than they expect you to. Remember your responsibility to your audience. They have other meetings to attend and duties to perform. Of course, if you are invited to continue beyond the time, fine, but plan to say what has to be said in the time allotted. Worse yet is when you are one of a series of speakers and each one runs three or four minutes longer than planned. Suppose you are scheduled as the last one before lunch. Think about it. Will stomachs rumble and lunch be delayed because you had to start late, or will you find yourself being asked to cut out 10 minutes of your talk because the caterers are scheduled to serve at 1.00 on the dot? Enough said! Watch the time!

"Who Else?"

What this question seeks to elicit is: will there be any other people speaking. If so, who and about what and in what sequence? The answer again assists you in selection of content. Be sure to request the time slot that you want. If you learn that, yes, the Managing Director will be speaking or the Tánaiste or Phil Collins, you probably will not want to be the next speaker, so find out the sequence of speakers and decide where you want to be placed in relation to each of them. In addition to who they are, what they are expected to talk about is important for you to know. For example, it is helpful to know in advance that the Financial Director will be talking about new cost-cutting measures, particularly if the subject of your talk involves increased expenditure. In other words, you need to be aware if the other speakers will have the same perspective that you have on a subject or opposing ones. Having this kind of information in advance will help you include or exclude material or underline certain concepts.

"How many?"

You are asking this question to help establish your pre-sentational style and perhaps the design of the talk as

well. Typically, the larger the group, the more formal you may want to be. It is possible, but more difficult, to be casual and interactive with 250 people in the room. By knowing how many will attend you can also begin to think about the type of visuals or handouts that you might need for those numbers and to plan when and what you will need designed, typed and/or photocopied. Maybe a flip chart will be sufficient with five people. Perhaps slides or other electronic media will be necessary for 200. Remember, do not take action yet. You are merely asking questions to collect data to help you make sensible decisions about your talk.

"Where?"

This question addresses both the location of the venue and of the specific room within it intended for your talk. If you learn that the talk is to be given in the conference room of the company where you work, that requires one kind of reconnaissance, but if you learn that the talk is to be given in the ballroom at a hotel in Limerick or Sligo and you live in Tralee, another type is required. If the event is off-site, and you have to travel some distance to get there, then there is additional time required for acclimatisation and to ensure that you have the equipment you need. If the presentation is in your own company's conference room, preparations will probably be less complicated, but you will still have to get to know the room, its strengths and limitations. Chapter 11 addresses in detail the importance of getting to know the venue.

"When?"

As with the other questions, your question is seeking more than one piece of information. On the one hand, you want to know the date of your talk so that you can determine how much time you have to get organised—two weeks, a month, tomorrow at 10 a.m.? In fact, based on what you hear, you may decide to say that you cannot do it. In a situation where you have been given too little time to prepare what you know constitutes a professional talk, then you may want to decline.

Your good name is at stake so that is the right decision. However, sometimes you can influence someone else's decision. Negotiate. "Tuesday is not possible but Thursday is," you might say. Whenever possible make choices about the timing that works for you. Naturally, if you are asked to speak at a board meeting that is scheduled for the third Thursday of every month, you will probably have no choice. But when you have options, take them.

For example, are you being asked to speak right after lunch? Do you want to? Analyse your working style. Do you concentrate better in the morning; therefore, are you a morning person? Do you feel more alert at 9.30 a.m. than at 3.00 p.m., or is the reverse true? In other words, find out as much as you can by asking "when", not only because of the implications the answer has for you personally but also because there may be design implications. Do you think that the mood of the audience on Tuesday morning after a bank holiday will be the same as on a Friday afternoon? You know how you feel in such a circumstance. Will you be speaking at the same time as a World Cup broadcast, or an All Ireland Hurling Final, or the final heats of the Olympics, or an Election or the Academy or Bafta Awards? Will the dead of winter or the brilliance of a summer day affect the motivation of the group? As soon as you know when, you decide what may interfere with your talk being heard or what you have to consider in order to have your message taken on board.

"Who?"

Because of the emphasis on audience, you already know that this is a key question. Remember the two-way communication process? The answer to "who" is going to assist you in understanding more about the receivers of your message and, therefore, what kind of codes should be selected for them. The answer to your question "how many?" has already given you the number in attendance. Now you are looking for more specific information about those individuals.

On one level, a demographic breakdown helps. What is the sex, age, education, nationality, work experience of the audience? Is English their first language? What are their job titles, what types of organisations or departments are they working in or what kinds of organisations do they belong to or represent—private, public, large, small, retail, financial? All of this kind of information is important whether the talk is being delivered within your own organisation or at a conference. Naturally, you will be more familiar with your own colleagues, but even so remember to ask who is going to be there: The Marketing Director? The head of R & D? All the PAs? The secretarial staff? Only the accountants?

If you can, find out some of the internal politics. Who has just been promoted? Who was bypassed? Who is counting the days to retirement? Who must attend the meeting but does not want to? Who is hostile? Who is looking for a promotion? In other words, the more you know about the group, the more accurately you will be able to select the appropriate data and anecdotes for your talk. You will also be able to eliminate what you believe is known by all. For example, if everyone has been in the industry or working in the company for five years or more, you may only have to provide a cursory review of the history of the new product line. If there is new staff, you may have to devote more time explaining the background. Or suppose your talk is primarily about the findings from some market research. It is helpful to know what your audience's comfort level is with certain terms and concepts in the field. If they are unfamiliar with the subject, you may need to include more basic information.

What you are doing is constantly seeking data to balance what your audience already knows and what it needs to know, so that you can make educated decisions about the degree of understanding the audience has about a given topic. In addition, you will also be getting a sense of their level of interest. If you discover that everyone is required to attend the meeting, you as a speaker may have a different motivational task than if you learn that they all chose to attend.

"Why all the demographic stuff if I know their job titles?" you ask. As you will see in Chapter 6, an effective talk is filled with real-life examples, images and anecdotes. Therefore, the more you know about the audience, the more accurate you can be in selecting these stories. Given what you know about a group's age, sex, job titles, nationality, you will be in a better position to decide if you can refer to Madonna, Maureen O'Hara, BMWs, Paris fashions, Grunge, Gazza, Senator Packwood, Marketshare, River Phoenix, Jacques Delors, a scrum, base hit or rugby, soccer, knitting or cooking. Will they know what or whom you are talking about when you make reference to such illustrations?

"What?"

This question concerns the content of your talk. When you pose it, the answer should clarify the theme, the content and the subject matter. Of course, the scope or depth of the talk will be affected by the amount of time you have to talk. Are you supposed to discuss the marketing plan for all the companies' products, or the plan for just one product in the line? Or are you to discuss one aspect of the plan for a particular product? If you learn that you are to explain a new policy, are you expected to include the rationale for the policy as well as the implementation, or are you only being asked to explain the content of the policy itself? In other words, the question "what?" sets the parameters of the talk. Until you have a complete answer to this question, though, your talk will have little impact or none at all.

"Why?"

This question goes beyond the content and is asked so that you can determine the purpose of the talk. Suppose the answer to your "what?" question was to talk about a new attendance policy. The next question, "why?", seeks to determine a rationale for the audience's knowing about the policy. In other words, you as a speaker have to articulate what you want them to do as a result of what you are telling them.

For example, do you want them to understand the new policy in order to avoid some kind of confusion? Do you want them simply to understand that there is a new policy? Do you want them to understand that there are grave implications if there are violations of the policy? Do you want them to understand those implications? Do you want them not to be concerned by the change of policy? Therefore, is the purpose to show how the new policy is not so different from the old one? Do you want them to see the benefits of the policy? Do you want to tell them about the new policy, so that they will be more accepting of it now that they have been invited to have information shared with them? Are they there to vote on the new policy? Are they there to debate it?

Any or all or more of those questions raise possibilities once you ask "what?" and then "why?". In essence, your question "why?" is asked to ensure that you and the audience know what the point of the talk is. It is your responsibility as a speaker to ensure that the audience knows why they are there and that they understand your point. They may not like what they hear, but if you have prepared well, they will understand what the subject was and why they heard it.

"How?"

This question seeks to determine the best method for making the presentation. Does the person who nominated you as the speaker already have a plan in mind? Is it to be a panel discussion? Would a question and answer approach be better? Are you being asked to talk for 20 minutes? Are you supposed to read a paper for 35 minutes? Some plans may already be in place, but you may decide that given the answers you have received to the what, the why and the who, the initial design will not work or be as effective; it may be boring or too structured or too interactive or too casual. It is clear that each one of these questions is separate, yet they are all interrelated. Talking for 45 minutes at 100 senior managers who are used to taking charge may not work. You will need to ponder what will. Suppose you learn that you need to design a presentation for 15 junior people. You want to involve them in a group discussion, but you know that you will need to reassure them when you have learned that three of their supervisors will be present also, thus making for a threatening atmosphere. You may have to figure out how to structure what you say to keep 30 people, including 25 engineers and five human resource people, interested in a talk on performance appraisal that is scheduled for 2.30 on Thursday. The solutions are up to you and your creativity.

As you gather the information based on the answers to the five 'w's—plus the additional five questions of how, how many, how long, who else and why not—you are making content decisions about what to say, how to say it and what not to say. You may also be asserting your own views based on your awareness of possible human conflicts or venue limitations. You may be negotiating for 5 or 10 minutes more or less, for a room that is bigger or smaller, or perhaps you are recommending that the talk should be given separately to two groups rather than one because of your conviction that the message can be coded and received more accurately doing it that way. You are now able to decide what you may want the participants to do and what you will do as well. Thus, by asking key questions and making recommendations for change based on the answers, you will be better able to move armed with invaluable information to the next phase of the process, the preparation of your speech.

Chapter 6

PREPARING YOUR SPEECH

"To communicate, put your thoughts in order; give
them a purpose; use them to persuade, to instruct,
to discover, to seduce."
—William Safire, columnist, *The New York Times*

"A speech is a solemn responsibility. The man who makes
a bad thirty-minute speech to 200 people wastes only a
half hour of his time. But he wastes 100 hours of the
audience's time—more than four days—which should be
a hanging offense."
—Jenkin Lloyd Jones, American writer

Let's now look at your speech, first in terms of selecting
data to support your message or purpose; second, in terms
of how best to organise it; and third, in terms of the actual
word choices that you make, some to include and some to
exclude.

Once you have asked and answered the questions listed
in the previous chapter, it is time to start collecting the
actual data that you will need for the talk itself so as to
make your point or points clearly, accurately and convinc-
ingly. It may require interviewing, researching or analysing.
And you will accumulate more information than you
need. However, too often, speakers, having gathered the
data, include all of it in the finished talk. The result is
information overload, or what we know as waffle. Instead,

with the subject and purpose of the talk clear in your own mind, sift through all the data you have, eliminating what may be tangential or charming but irrelevant.

Select only the information that establishes the context and supports your arguments for the position you are espousing. If you have material on the construction of the Sligo plant, the subject of your talk, and you have found data on the one in Tipperary, be brave and file the Tipperary information for a future talk, if it is not relevant to this one.

How you initially organise that mass of data is up to you. You probably have developed an efficient organising technique at this point. Some people like to make lists of bullet points or write random thoughts on sheets of paper. Others prefer to outline their thoughts. Still others write headings and group relevant ideas under each one. Putting your thoughts together for a talk is no different from organising your ideas for a written report, so select whatever method works well for you. What is important is that you go through the process and create a preliminary structure.

It is important to remember that you are constrained in your talk by the necessity of relying on verbal clarity. There is no next paragraph or appendix for the reader to

read, or to go back and reread, for that matter. You are
also constrained by the amount of time you have to discuss your subject. Therefore, you have to be sure to select
only that information that keeps you on target.

By having asked all the preparation questions, you
should have a good idea about the audience's level of
knowledge about your topic as well as their frame of
reference. Because of that, you can decide what terms, if
any, need to be defined or how much of the context must
be clarified for them. Suppose you are to discuss the
results of a recent safety audit. If your preliminary questioning establishes that your audience already knows
about the audit, you will not need to devote time explaining
the history of the audit and who carried it out. Instead,
you will be able to concentrate on discussing only the
findings of the audit and the subsequent implications for
the audience in front of you.

Of course, it is always more difficult to gauge what is
essential to include in a talk when you have a diverse
group coming from different departments or backgrounds.
What may be old hat to the financial people, may be new
to the members of the R & D department or vice versa.
Their perspectives on issues may be equally varied, so you
need to seek a balance that neither ignores one group nor
demeans another. Sometimes the best way to do that is
simply to acknowledge orally the degree of diversity. This
could be as simple as, "Although most of you are familiar
with _____, let me clarify _____".

You know what the subject is and why you are talking
about it. You have collected the essential and eliminated
the nonessential data on the topic. By putting the audience foremost in your mind, you should now begin to
anticipate some of their questions or arguments about the
subject matter. Sales people sometimes call this process,

"overcoming objections". To prepare, you need to think through the topic and examine it from the audience's perspective. You then build their arguments and objections into your speech. You might say, for example, "Some of you may be wondering why we need a new policy at all, when the previous _____", and then proceed to explain why; or you could indicate that you know that "Some of you may have questions, which I will answer later." Once again, your audience must stay foremost in your thoughts.

The Structure

So far, you have asked, gathered, included, excluded, added, and deleted possible key ideas and finally identified those that are vital to making your position clear in your talk. It is time, now, to refine the initial structure for the speech and to organise the material within it. The questions that you asked in preparation came as no surprise to you. This next step should not surprise you either. The talk needs a beginning, a middle and an end. It is important to remember, however, what you expect to accomplish in each of the sections.

The beginning of the talk is designed to get the audience's attention, to focus their thoughts on you and on what you are saying. It is the part of the speech in which you state the objectives of the talk, sometimes including its length and the approach that you plan to use. "During the next 20 minutes," you might say, "we will review point by point the _____". You might also include the limitations; that is, you could explain what you are not going to talk about, so they have no expectations about those ideas: "I will only be talking about _____, not _____".

The middle of the talk restates your points and gives you the opportunity to elaborate on each of your arguments or ideas. It is the heart of the speech and must include all the supporting data you have accumulated.

The end of the talk restates your original objective and may also ask the audience to take some kind of action based on what you have said. For example, suppose that you state in the beginning that the objective of the talk is to give X number of reasons why Ireland is an ideal tourist destination. Then in the closing, when you restate your objective, you tell the audience what you want them to do: visit, tell their relatives, read a book, consider a bus tour, change their plans or bring their golf clubs. You are stating clearly what it is that you want from them. Thus, they leave the room with that message clearly in their minds.

The Beginning

Even though you will write your opening last, let's talk about it here. If part of the intent of your talk's beginning is to be motivational and to have people focus on you and your words, then let's look at some of the methods by which you can coax people to take their minds off their other responsibilities and to listen to you.

The most straightforward approach is to state your objective: "Smoking is considered a health hazard, and today we will review the current medical findings." There are other techniques for opening sentences that you may want to use. For example, you may want to begin with a quotation, "Jack Charlton said '_____'," or you may tell a story or an anecdote: "A few years ago _____" or "The last time I spoke in _____" or "There is a wonderful story _____". If you are a good joke teller, you may want to try humour as an approach. Jokes, though, can be worrisome, because no matter how witty you are the audience may not be amused. If you are not feeling confident to begin with, and your audience does not laugh, then the initial setback may only make you feel more uncomfortable.

Another way to begin a talk is with a question: "Do you _____?" or "Have you _____?" or "How many of you _____?" Yet another technique is the use of a statistic or a shocking fact. A now famous opener was used by a Professor of Medicine who gazed out at his first year students and asked them to look first to their right and then to their left, "because", he said "only one out of the three of you will be sitting here on the first day of term next year". You can be certain that he got their attention!

Some people can use dramatic approaches: make strange noises, throw things, wear shocking clothing, burst balloons, but that kind of approach works for some, not for all. The downside risk of that kind of theatricality is that the audience may remember the balloons but not the talk that followed their bursting.

As you can see, you have a variety of options to choose from. The choices for opening lines are limited only by your imagination, so you may want to experiment with different styles to determine what works for you.

The Middle

As you structure the middle of your talk, it is vital to remember what we said earlier about inattentiveness being a barrier to effective communication. As you design your presentation, repeat key words, ideas or phrases. Virtually every TV commercial illustrates this, because new ideas are fragile, like new behaviours such as trying not to say "em". Until the idea is ingrained the listener may forget, so you need to repeat your key points. Remember how you were taught vocabulary as a youngster or when you were learning another language? Repetition. Repetition.

Repetition. Bear that experience in mind when you prepare your talk.

The heart of the matter is the middle. It is in this section of your speech that you develop the arguments, positions or explanations that you indicated at the start you were going to talk about. Suppose, as we said earlier, that you have been asked to talk about why Ireland is an ideal tourist destination. You have told the audience in the beginning that there are 10 reasons. In the body of the talk you develop or explain each one of the 10.

In other talks you may not have a list, but instead have a process to describe or the stages or phases of a plan to explain, for example, "The new recruiting process has five steps". In the middle of the talk you explain, clarify, justify each of the five steps in a logical sequence. You may be giving a talk in which you are arguing for and against something, the pros and cons, for example, of buying new equipment. In this instance, you may organise the middle by discussing all five positives first and then the five negatives, or one pro and then one con, then the next pro and the next con, and so on. Regardless of your approach, you must create a logical sequence.

Suppose you have five arguments to support your recommendation for buying the equipment. You need to decide in what order to put each of the five; which is number one, and which are numbers two, three, four and five? Make a decision about the sequence. Do not just let the order happen because it was in the order in which you collected the data. Do you want the most important reason first? Do you want it last? That decision affects where the least important reason goes, first or last. Which arguments do you want in the middle of your list? In what order? Why?

Maybe the subject of your talk, your five-year-plan, perhaps, has to do with what was, what is and what will be.

Then a natural sequence might be chronological order—
past to present to future. Or do you want to work in the
opposite direction, future to past? When you make your
decision about sequence, it is important to remember that
the audience is being asked to recall information primarily
by hearing. In the absence of a script, numbered lists and
sequenced information will assist them in following your
train of thought as well as helping them to retain it.

But numbering is not always possible or appropriate.
Suppose, for example, you want to explain a theoretical
construct. Theory is abstract; it is difficult to visualise; it
is intangible, so it is essential that you give the audience
an example of the theory at work or an example of its
application. Remember Maslow's Hierarchy of Needs? It
is invariably pictured as a pyramid, a device that helps
you to visualise the concept. The top of the pyramid is
usually labelled self-actualisation. But what does that
mean? You cannot hold self-actualisation or touch it. So,
if you think back to the first time you met that particular

pyramid, either the author or the instructor gave you examples of what self-actualisation means to real people or asked what it meant to you. In other words, it is important to describe a theoretical concept with an image or an example. You can talk about an internal combustion engine, or you can show a picture of one. You can discuss strategic planning, but it helps to visualise it. You can talk about information technology, but you need to give the audience something to hold on to either in the form of an image, application, example or analogy. Imagine trying to persuade tourists to visit Ireland without showing them any pictures of the beauty spots.

Suppose your talk is not about theory, but about the layout of an office building. Perhaps you will decide to organise your talk spatially, moving from the description of the left side of the building, then to the right, or from the top to the bottom or from the bottom to the top. What you are doing is planning your talk to enable the audience to follow your verbal logic. The talk could be sequenced to discuss the macro issues first and then the micro ones. What if the subject is geographical? Do you want it organised in terms of East to West or West to East or North to South or the reverse?

If none of these approaches fits the subject of the talk then you need to look for other methods of organising the data. But find one. Could it be in terms of threats and opportunities? In terms of similarities and differences? Could you raise several questions and then answer each one in turn?

Numbering is always useful. It helps the audience take notes, to say nothing of the fact that you have fingers on your hands that might be useful. Be sure, though, that if you decide to use numbers you do so consistently. If you say that you have five points, do not mention number one, number two and number four and forget to say the number three. Invariably the members of the audience will check with their neighbours to find out what happened to number three. They will be talking to each other not listening to you.

Another mechanism for creating internal structure is by using memory aids, mnemonics. As you organise your thoughts, you will discover that certain key words or ideas stand out. When you write them down, note the first letter of each word. Can you make a word from those letters that will help the audience remember your key ideas? For example, "Today we are examining a DREAM." You then explain that the letter D stands for development, R for reason and so on. Each letter represents one of the points that you want to make. Are you familiar with AIDA in selling? Each letter stands for a key concept—attention, interest, desire, action. ABC is another: Always Be Closing. The objective of using the mnemonic is to help the listener remember the points. As always there is a caveat: be careful that your mnemonic is not too long; for example, ENVIRONMENT, E = energy, N = nature, V = vegetation, etc. The audience may only remember the mnemonic and not what it stands for.

To recap: by now you have finished preparing the middle of your talk and have determined what you are going to say, why you are going to say it and what data you plan to use to substantiate your arguments. In so doing, you have eliminated certain material because it may have been merely tangential or too long. Therefore, go back to the opening, which is designed to motivate the audience to listen and to establish the objectives. You may also decide to tell them what you are not going to include. In research that is often called the "limitations of the study". What that means is that you are telling the audience precisely what the parameters are, and therefore letting them know what they should not expect to hear. In that way you narrow their focus and expectations to only the points that you plan to talk about. They will not anticipate more than that.

For example, suppose you are going to talk about a current appraisal system. You may indicate that you are speaking only about the one for the secretarial staff, not the one for the technical staff, or you may indicate that you are speaking only about the system that has been in place for the past three years, not the older one. If 10 reasons for visiting Ireland is the subject, you may say that this is limited to the Autumn and the Spring, or for the visitor who is over 35. In that way you clarify precisely for the audience what your topic is.

The Closing

Finally, let's look at closing lines. In essence, you have exactly the same choices for ending a talk as you do for beginning one. For example, suppose you chose to start the talk with a Jack Charlton quotation; you might then want to end it with the same one or one by Franz Beckenbauer. Suppose you decided to begin by asking a question; you might consider ending with the answer to the opening question, or restating the original one or asking yet another one. Start with a story, end with a story. Start with a statistic, close with one. What is important to realise is that once again you have to make a decision in advance. People remember the beginnings and ends of talks better than they remember the middles, so you need to find an effective way to grab their attention at the outset and then to remind them at the end of what you told them and what you want from them. Those aspects are too important to be left to chance.

This then is the organisation of the talk. So far so good: a beginning with a solid appropriate attention-getting device, a statement of the objectives, explanation of the limitations followed by a middle which is logically sequenced, then a closing that restates your objectives—the what-and-why you were talking about the subject. What you have done is outline the talk. It is a strong skeleton but now you have to flesh it out with words and examples. How do you do that?

Specificity

First of all, be specific, whenever possible. When you choose words like "huge", "tremendous", "great", "wonderful", "vast", "costly", "enormous", the audience has no frame of reference. Is it as "vast" as the Phoenix Park or the Sahara Desert? In other words, my idea of "huge" may be different from yours. What is "costly" to me may be a pittance to you. Is a "stack" of post a foot deep or an inch deep? Therefore, use specifics: 15 per cent, £4, next Tuesday, what improvements exactly, not "significant" ones. The more specific you can be, the less your audience will suffer from waffle. Look at all the quiz shows that proliferate because of our ability to retain specifics. How did James Bond take his martini: "Shaken, not _____"?

Analogies

Another useful tool is to make analogies or use examples that bring your subject to life. Is the budget equivalent to the national debt? Were the hail stones the size of golf balls? Was the office so crowded it looked like Bewley's on a Saturday morning? Were the people so delighted they looked like Packie Bonner after he had made another save? Was it so hot that you could cook eggs on the road? In other words, whenever possible, provide verbal images, specifics or analogies.

Word Choice

It is impossible here to review every word or phrase you might use in a talk; however, let's examine some of the frequently selected words and phrases that you should consider eliminating in the same way that there are certain gestures or other movements that detract from your presentation and should be avoided.

Let's eliminate a group of them quickly. Those are words or phrases that may be inappropriate, clever or sarcastic, remarks that are demeaning, insulting or stereotyping and touch on such items as: sex, job, age, religion, ethnic background, politics and disability. You know the list, but in preparing your talk you need to double check that you have not slipped something into your talk by mistake. It is easy to offend, and when you do, you risk alienating someone who may be a member of a particular group or related to someone who is or who may have strong feelings on the subject.

When you refer to secretaries as "girls" or managers as "he's" or "over 50's" as sedentary, you risk offending. Let the audience make the snide comment about a recent political faux pas in some country; don't you do it. An inappropriate reference may cost you a member of the audience. He or she may focus on the remark, think about it and either lose the flow of the talk or, worse yet, resent you because you have enunciated values that are incompatible with theirs. It is an expensive error. Let's be clear that what is being referred to is your choice of examples or asides. The subject matter itself may be difficult for some people to take, such as, redundancy. But be careful of inadvertent insults.

Be mindful, too, when you select your supporting data, of saying something that is wrong, inaccurate, illegal or unethical. Suppose, for example that you cite references to events that you think occurred in 1989. In fact, they occurred in 1991. There will surely be someone in the audience who is aware of the error and will see a crack in your credibility. You will have a difficult time regaining it. If one statistic is wrong, will there be others?

You will probably be ready to run through your talk now, so as you do, another recommendation about word choice involves less dangerous ground than offending or making factual mistakes. Some words are just annoying or distracting. They are single words, analogies or phrases like "as you know," "at this stage," "as such," "OK," "well," "right". Nothing wrong with any one of them, but you would be amazed at how many times a pet phrase is sprinkled throughout a talk without the speaker realising. These words and phrases only constitute a problem when they are used with such frequency that the audience notices them and begins to count. For example, if you say "OK" at the end of every sentence or every time you change an acetate, you may find that the audience is beginning to keep track on the corner of their notes. It is important to notice if you do have the tendency to repeat certain expressions because you risk the audience beginning to focus on them, not on the rest of your talk. Catch yourself, if you are in the habit of starting a sentence with "well" or "right"! Think of the wasted effort. All that time you devoted to finding the right opening words and then ruining things with "well"! You cure yourself the same way that you are curing yourself of other habits: catch yourself doing it and then gradually decrease its use.

Another caveat about phrases: watch out for the self-deprecating ones: "I hope that I did not bore you," or "I am *just* going to talk about _____" or "I am *only* going to take a few minutes," or, when you close, "well, that's it!" After all that work, organising, structuring, looking for examples and analogies, what are you apologising for? You may think the phrases or words are endearing. In fact, they can have a negative effect. Before there is any misunderstanding, the phrase "I am just going to talk about _____" is very different from telling a story on yourself, about a mistake you made or weight that you have gained over the holidays. Revealing a foible can be charming, and may help establish rapport. You should not apologise for work, however. If you have taken the responsibility for the talk, be proud and own the moment. Make no apologies.

There is another specific sentence that you should avoid using. Many presentations begin with "Today I am going to talk about _____". Eliminate that phrase and instead plunge right into the talk. For example, instead of "I am going to talk about the importance of increasing our _____", try "Increasing our ____ is important." It is more direct. While we are at it, think, too, about whether it's "I" or "we". "I" separates; "we" joins. So, if you believe that your message will be received better with "we", by all means use it.

There are two additional points: one about "finally", the other about "thank you". "Finally" or "In conclusion" should be said only once, when your talk is almost over. You are signalling to the audience that you are finished. Many speakers say "finally" then keep on talking and add "and, my last point is ____," and keep on talking and add, "so, in summary ____" and keep on talking and add, "therefore, to conclude ____". End your talk once.

And then there is "Thank you". The objective of the final sentence in your talk is to reinforce your main points or underline your message, so take care not to let your "thank you" slide into the final words. Say your final sentence. Take a pause. What usually happens is that you receive a well-earned round of applause, or you will be thanked by some key person on behalf of the others present. *They*, not you, say "thank you" with their applause. You, however, then thank them for their expression of gratitude, be it applause or kind words. Why all the fuss about such a simple point? It is a pity to hear a well-thought out final thought blurred by closing amenities. Say what you have to say, pause or stop, and then acknowledge the applause. You will have earned it!

In summary, having asked your questions, you assemble the data, bearing your purpose and audience in mind. You then organise your talk into three sections, carefully sequencing the middle so as to aid retention. Both the beginning and the end state your message and ensure that attention is being paid. Once you have drafted your talk, you look for ways to bring in analogies and specifics, ensuring that they are accurate and not offensive. Having drafted the talk, you will be beginning to practise so take care not to include extraneous words and remarks that, like inappropriate body language, detract from your key ideas.

Chapter 7

USING NOTES

"William Graham spoke without a note, and almost
without a point."
—Winston Churchill

Now that your talk has been thought through and drafted,
it is time to make yet another decision about your notes.
This chapter addresses the importance of notes, and how
to use note cards as prompts. We will not be discussing
electronic options, such as teleprompters.

In essence, you now have to decide whether to write the
talk out in long hand, type it on A4 paper and then read it
out word for word, or whether to jot notes on paper or on
cards and then speak extemporaneously. You may decide
that you are going to memorise the whole talk. There are
those who believe that a talk should be memorised. Having
already read about my fiasco of years ago, you know that
I would advise against relying on your memory. The
downside risk is enormous. If anything goes wrong that
causes you to lose your train of thought, or that causes you
to become unduly anxious, then the worst can happen—
and your doubts will be realised—you may forget it all. If
you ask other speakers, you will discover that memory
lapse does happen to speakers at one time or another. It is
possible to look at the audience and to panic. Not to worry;
it does not happen often, but it can, so unless you have a
masochistic need to experience that disaster, decide to use

notes of some kind. Having notes humanises you, too, in the eyes of the audience and makes you more credible.

Reading Versus Using Notes

Before looking more closely at what you write down for notes, let's return to the notion of reading the speech. You often see that approach at professional conferences where presenters "deliver a paper". Reading papers is not about establishing rapport; it is hard to establish any eye contact, to weigh reactions and thus, to alter pace, pitch, volume or content. Try reading this page as if there were an audience. Notice that when you look up from the page to look at the audience, it is easy to lose your place, and then your poise.

Reading a paper also makes you more dependent on a lectern, because you need to put the papers on something. If you hold them in your hands, the pages are quite awkward, particularly as you read near the bottom or turn the pages. Paper is noisy and if there is a mike, all in the room will hear sheets of paper crackle. If you do decide to

read, be sure to use good quality paper and not pages torn from a refill pad. You have seen that, and it is not a pretty sight. It may give the impression that you wrote the talk on the way over to the meeting. The audience needs to know you have invested time in them.

Some presenters use their overheads or slides as prompts or notes. We will be discussing visuals in the next chapter, but using slides as prompts raises some more questions. You need to ask yourself whether the visuals were designed for you or for the audience. Is there too much written on them? Did you have to use too many of them, because they are your notes? Or are you speaking without notes until you turn on your first overhead or slide? In other words, unless you are striking some kind of balance, you could leave yourself vulnerable at first without any prompts, or have too many slides or sentences because you need too many prompts.

It is far better to use notes and to use record cards for your notes. Why record cards? Paper, as noted previously, is awkward and noisy; 3" × 5" or 4" × 6" cards are not. They can fit in your hand and they also fit in a pocket, which means you can carry them and practise conveniently. And unless you shuffle them they will not make any noise.

Using Note Cards

What do you put on the cards? First of all, you should write on only one side of the card, and then number them in sequence, just in case they become disordered. Write in letters large enough to enable you to see them if you were holding them at arm's length. On each card you might write one of your key ideas, justifications or rationales. After the key idea should be the word or words to remind you of the examples that you plan to use to bring that idea to life.

> 4.The climate of Ireland
> —maritime
> —temperate
> —changeable

If you have a new idea later, all you have to do is add a card or destroy one. You do not have to retype the whole speech or squeeze in your ideas on the margin of the paper. You may want one card with the opening completely written out. That is extra insurance at the beginning when you are at your most anxious and might want the additional support. In addition to your cards with the key ideas, you may also want to reproduce your slides or acetates onto your cards. In that way you will not have to turn your back to the audience when you show them. The words on the slide will be in your hand as well as reproduced on the screen.

Practising with Notes

Now you need to begin to practise your talk using your note cards. As you do, you will notice that there are a number of other advantages to using note cards besides the

fact that they are noiseless and fit in your pockets. During your talk, they allow you to be more mobile. Remember that sheets of paper keep you near the lectern, and that is not always desirable. The only support the cards need is from your hands, so you are freer to move around the room. In addition, the cards give you something to do with your hands, thus taking care of one or two of those extra appendages that appeared when you walked to the front. In addition, you can hold your hands in such a way that a quick glance at your notes is all that is needed for you to continue, down and up. Thus you break your eye contact with the audience only briefly.

If you have never used them before, it takes time to adjust to using cards. Two points, as you practise: if you know that you have the habit of holding your hands together as you speak, do not hold on to the cards in the same way. One hand should hold the pack, the other may hold the card that you are referring to and then moves it to the bottom of the pack when you are finished with it. And the second recommendation: try not to fidget with the cards, to turn them around or to tap with them. If you do, then your notes themselves become a distraction. When you have read your note, please do not throw the finished card on the nearest table as if you cannot wait to be rid of it. Hold them all with pride. Remember, they represent hours of work reduced to a pack of 3" × 5" record cards.

As you become more used to working with notes you may find them reassuring, too. With your key words written down, you eliminate the fear of blanking out, you know what you are going to say. Notes also serve to bring you back on track, if you are distracted by someone or something in the audience. Perhaps someone asked a question or you thought of a good story to tell. Notes will remind you where you left off and where you still need to go to get your message across.

Chapter 8

USING VISUALS AND HANDOUTS

"Visuals act as punctuation points in your presentation.
They offer relief to the audience and make the audience's
commitment a series of short decisions to stay tuned
instead of one long, unattractive obligation."
—Ed Brenner, photographer and publisher

"A picture may instantly present what a book could
set forth only in a hundred pages."
—Ivan Turgenev

Visuals have been referred to several times before. This
chapter is dedicated to them because they warrant more
than a passing reference. Visuals are used to assist the
audience in retaining and understanding information.
When you both see and hear about something at the same
time, it will stay in your mind longer. For example, you
can describe your house verbally to an audience, but by
giving them a picture and talking about it simultaneously
you will give your audience a far better sense of what you
want them to see. You can talk about Daniel Day-Lewis'
portrayal of Christy Brown, or you can show a photograph
as you speak. The impact is different. That is why you use
visuals. They can be words, pictures, graphs, charts or
props. Let's consider them separately, along with handouts.

Once your talk is outlined, and your key points and supporting examples for each thought through carefully, it is time to review your speech and determine where a visual would clarify a point or reinforce your words, and what kind of visual would accomplish that best. Remember you do not use graphics just because you think every talk requires them. You use them because they make a difference. Often a presentation is a follow-up to a study or report, so speakers use the report itself as the basis for the talk. Unfortunately, the visuals are too often actual copies of pages taken out of the report, either from the appendix or from the findings. The problem is that that is what the visuals look like—pages from a report with page numbers and all.

It is important to remember that written documents are different from talks. One difference is that reports can be read over time by an individual in isolation, re-read, read in sections, put down, and picked up again. Because the reader can pore over it at leisure, a table or a chart in a report can be more detailed and have smaller print than

one in a talk. An audience does not have that luxury. In essence, you cannot necessarily use a visual that was designed for another medium. To repeat: you have to decide what the audience needs to see and how you want them to see it.

But before examining what a good visual looks like, you need to decide what kind of visuals would be appropriate. When you do that you have to factor in the number of people present in the room. Do you want them to have a handout at the end when they leave the room? Do you think that it would be better for them to have some written material before you start? Is there no need at all for slides, videos, handouts, or pre-printed acetates because you feel that writing on a white board as you talk is better? Will a flip chart do? You make the decisions based on such considerations as: the degree of formality, the purpose of the talk, the nature of the topic, the size of the room and number of people. Certainly videos and slides are both expensive and time consuming to produce, while creating your own visual clarification or reinforcements with a white board or flip chart is more immediate and casual. Another inexpensive option is to "pre-flip" or write on the board in advance of your talk.

Let's suppose you have decided that you need one slide or overhead with the title of your talk and then one for each of your key points. In addition, you might use one or two more for charts or graphs in order to demonstrate a particular trend that supports your argument, a picture of the product you are discussing, and a map indicating some demographic data. Let's examine what you should take into consideration when you design these graphics. First of all, any slide primarily devoted to words should be kept simple and should have print large enough and dark enough against the background for everyone in the room to see it. You should also have a generous amount of "white space" around the margins and between the points, so that the slide is easy to read from anywhere in the room. Avoid complete sentences; instead, use phrases or bullet points. If you use bullet points, be sure that the language of each point is consistent. Look at this:

The purpose of the research was to:
- determine the _____
- assess the _____
- conclusions about the _____

Notice that this speaker begins each of the first two points with a verb, "determine" and "assess", and the third point with a noun, "conclusions." The third item in the list should, in fact, also be a verb, "conclude". Alternatively, the first two points should become nouns instead, "determination" and "assessment". Then, of course, you would have to change the stem as well: "The purpose of the research was to make _____." This makes it easier for the audience to follow. Be sure, too, that the points on your graphic are lined up under each other, not two spaces to the left:

- determine the _____
- assess the _____
  - conclude that _____
  - recommend that _____

Such carelessness not only looks sloppy, but it also distracts your audience. Inconsistent use of upper and lower case is equally annoying:

- Determine the _____
- assess the _____
- Conclude that _____

Do not forget to proof-read for typographical errors: "invoolment", "accomodation", "liason", missing or misplaced apostrophes. A typo signals to the audience that you are inattentive to detail. They may wonder if you did not have time to check on these points and that perhaps some of your other research, remarks or recommendations are also sloppy. If the audience allows that possibility to enter their minds, there goes your credibility. If you are under great time constraints, better not to use visuals than have any that are less than excellent.

Besides ensuring that you have a good layout, consistent language and no typos, have a title or label indicating what the acetate is about, particularly with your charts and graphs. Too often, speakers spend time creating an excellent visual representation but forget to label it. Bear in mind that people can be distracted by a noise or may come into the room late. What a pity to have an exquisitely designed pie chart on the screen with percentages carefully indicating each segment, but the audience will not know what the figures represent because there is no title. So, label your graphics, especially if you are showing more than one chart or graph.

Suppose you have decided to use a graph in order to demonstrate a trend. It, too, needs to be labelled and titled. You may find that the audience follows your train of thought better if you have one graph showing the basic data, the axis, then another to show the changes by overlaying the new information. In that way, the audience can grasp the information bit by bit while you assist them by providing the information in a systematic way.

To highlight a point in your visual, you may want to put an arrow next to a critical bar in the graph or put a circle around a key intersection. During the presentation you may use a pointer, remembering never to point it at the

audience. You tell them where you want them to look: "If you look at the last column on the right _____" or "Look at the top of the slide _____." Guide their eyes to the place that you want them to look; otherwise they will be taking in the information as they choose, not as you wish them to.

Also, look for logical sequences on your visuals, just as you did in the body of the talk. Numbers and years need careful organising. Stay chronological, if you can: 1990-91, 1991–92 not 1993–94, 1991–92, 1992–93. Write North to South, smallest to largest, largest to smallest, left to right.

Do not forget that if you give the audience something to read on a screen or in their hands, they will read it. Therefore, if it is an acetate, here is an opportunity for you to practise your pausing ability by giving them time to read it. In the same way you have talked them through a graph or map or chart, if there are words on the visual you guide them through by speaking the same words that are written on the screen as bullets. When you speak the words that are on the screen, the audience both hears and sees them. Thus, you are reinforcing your ideas and increasing the odds of the audience's retaining the information that you want them to remember.

Keep the visuals simple, though. If you have "10 Reasons for Making Ireland a Tourist Destination" all on one slide, while you are talking about number two the audience may be reading numbers nine and ten. You lose the reinforcement potential that way. That is why some speakers use the "revealing technique" by showing only part of the overhead at a time. Not everyone likes that approach. For some it is demeaning or childish. Once again, consider using more slides or acetates, or building them up by overlying acetates, turning the overhead or projector off between points.

Remember, too, that when you are using visuals you should not turn to the screen to look at them. Maintain eye contact with the audience. You do not abdicate that responsibility once you include images in your talk. If you are using a screen, stand to one side. Remember, reference to the image is on your cards. If you are using acetates, the picture is lying in front of you on the projector. Therefore, there is no reason for you to turn your back. You can see exactly what your audience is seeing simply by looking at the plate on which the acetate is lying. You need only to turn back quickly to look at the screen to ensure that the acetate is not at an angle or that it is right side up.

If you are using a flip chart or writing on an overhead, do not talk and write at the same time. If you do, you will be projecting your voice back to the board or down to the chart. Say the words and then turn to write them, or write them and then turn back to the audience and say them.

By the way, know your equipment. Know your equipment well. In Chapter 10, when we talk about practising, we will say more about this, but it is important to make the point twice now.

Earlier we mentioned that people will read whatever you distribute to them. So, if you have decided on using a handout at the beginning of the presentation, know that

people will read what you have given them. Build that factor into your plan: "If you look at the second point on the sheet, you will see that it says _____". In other words, control what they do with what you have distributed. Most people write on handouts so be sure that you have provided enough "white space" on the paper for them to jot down their notes. Suppose, however, you want each member of the audience to have a copy of a complex table. Give it to them at the time that they need to refer to it and then specify what aspect you want them to look at, once again "If you look at the third column, you will notice that it compares _____".

To avoid problems—the third person in the fifth row may not have received one, for example—handouts are usually distributed at the end of a talk or are placed at each seat before the audience arrives. If you decide to use replicas or mock ups, your responsibility is once again to ask yourself, just as you do with handouts or other visuals, what you are using them for and whether the audience will understand them and benefit from their use.

In other words, once again you have a plethora of options to choose from. You need to remember that the purpose of an image is to clarify and/or reinforce your message, so you need to select the best medium for the particular presentation and then ensure clarity and accuracy.

Chapter 9

HANDLING QUESTIONS

---

*"I'll answer some of your questions, the more
difficult ones will be answered by my colleagues."*
—Professor Roland Smith, Chairman, British Aerospace plc.

Tired? You should be. You have done a lot of work, and it
is almost time for the show to begin. You have asked
questions, planned your talk and identified what, if any,
visual reinforcement or clarification is required. By now
you have also decided what you are going to wear. Before
you go out there to face your public, you need to do more
thinking about one other aspect of your talk. This chapter
focuses on the time when you have ended your prepared
speech and you become the receiver. It is question time.
In fact there are some presentations that are all questions.
In planning your talk, you will have anticipated questions
and/or objections, and tried to understand the politics of
the audience as well, so you will have a good sense of
people's perspectives. However, people will ask what they
want to ask. The single most important recommendation
is to maintain control of the event. Do not let it slip away
from you.

Knowing your subject as you do, any question about
the content should be no problem for you. A good way to
prepare is to answer a few questions that a colleague or
friend poses. Before you do that, however, it is time for
more decisions. Do you want questions? If so, when? Are
they already built in to the design—for example, five

minutes at the end? Would you prefer to take some during the talk? If so, have you written yourself a note on your cards indicating that you need to tell the audience in the beginning that you will take questions during the talk? Maybe you have decided that questions will be over coffee, or that there will be no time for questions at all. Like so much else in presentation, you must make a decision about what works for the subject and for that audience.

Let's assume that you want to take questions and that rather than use an interactive approach, you want all the questions held until the end of your talk. How much time have you allotted for them? Ten minutes? Stick to that time. It is easy to lose control of the timing in this section of the presentation because one question or answer may lead to three or four more, so keep an eye on your watch

You have ended your talk with a solid closing. You have restated your objective and called the audience to action: "Starting Tuesday, we will all be ＿＿＿, because you can see we will be saving at least 10 per cent ＿＿＿." Applause! Thank you! Pause. Change of pace, perhaps of location, you move to the right, "Are there any questions?" or "I will

be delighted to take some questions" or "We have time for only three questions." You invite questions, and you do so with a smile on your face. This is not the time to look defensive. It is not the time to cross your arms on your chest and take two steps backward. It is the time to smile, to walk forward, to look open, eager and willing to take questions.

Let's take a moment to think about how it feels to be in the audience. You have been there. Think about what most people do in an audience when it is question time. They spend time formulating the question, finding the right words. Asking a question in a room full of people is a form of mini-presentation for the questioner. Therefore, people who ask questions need to be supported, so show some empathy, please. Think of the times that you have sat in an audience wanting to ask a question, but reluctant to do so, fearful that you will sound stupid or that you will appear not to have been listening. Your supervisor could be in the room seeing you make a fool of yourself. With those memories in your mind, be warm and gracious. No matter what you are asked, help the questioners retain their dignity. They will not articulate their gratitude to you, because they will not know that you are being empathetic, but they will appreciate your kindness and like you for it; that cannot hurt.

Frequently, questions have more to do with the questioner's need to be heard than they have to do with your talk. A little posturing may be involved. How often have you heard a questioner end up telling a story or saying "I just wanted to say ____" and then going on at length and never asking a question? If that happens, be sure that you are listening. There may be a question after the preamble. Do not daydream or replay your talk. It is not over yet. And listen, use your skills—maintain eye contact, nod, if

appropriate, to show that you are listening. Then be sure
that you understand the question. You may have to say,
"Do I understand you to mean _____?" Or you may want
to repeat the question, bearing in mind that a question
asked by someone in the front row may not be heard at
the back of the room. Or you may want to paraphrase the
question in words that are of your own choosing. The questioner says, "Aren't the implications catastrophic _____?"
You may want to select less emotive words: "The implications have an impact _____."

When you answer the question, do not respond only to
the questioner; address the room. You still have an obligation to everyone, and answering the question may give
you the opportunity to reinforce a point or clarify a misunderstanding. Try not to end up in a conversation or
dialogue with one person. In fact, if the question does
reinforce a point for you, then for heaven's sake, thank the
individual who asked it for raising the question, rather
than look angry or disgusted.

In addition, try not to make each of your answers too
long. Just answer the question. If you have got time for
only three questions, you should not devote the entire
time to one. Others will resent it. By the way, if you know
someone's name, by all means use it. Ask if there are more
questions, wait briefly. If there are none, simply thank the
audience, smile and go. *You* make the decision to end the
session.

If you get a hostile questioner, do not engage in combat.
Do not be dragged into a fight. Keep your answers on a
higher plain. Restate your points. But do not become rude.
Usually, aggressive questioners will embarrass themselves.

Suppose you get a question, and you have not a clue
what the answer to it is. It happens, but this is not the time
for fiction. If what you are concerned with is maintaining

or achieving your credibility, then do not lie or waffle. There is no available data on presenters who have been struck dead by a thunderbolt for not knowing the answers to every question. You are not expected to be omniscient; however, you are capable of finding out the answer. Being able to locate information is an important managerial skill, so admit that you do not have the answer but that you can find it. Thank the questioner for asking it and promise to get back to him/her with the answer. Be sure that you do!

If you have generated enthusiasm and an animated discussion ensues, it is important to maintain control. For example, if you do not know the answer to a question, person A may offer to answer person B and then person C might add to the discussion. What happens is that a discussion may develop among the members of the audience, which may be wonderful, but unless you lead it like a conductor you will be left standing, looking on. In other words, if you want A to talk to B and C to add something, be sure that *you*, not A, B, or C, are determining when they have said enough. *You* invite D to speak, not watch while D chimes in. When you decide that the debate has gone on long enough, you end it.

Sometimes it is interesting to have the debate move away from you, because it allows members of the audience to get involved. You may get some useful feedback from what they are saying. And such interaction will indicate that you have created enough interest to have sparked some dialogue. Good for you! Do not discourage it; just orchestrate it.

You have checked your watch. You indicate that time is up. You may or may not want to restate your closing remarks. You hold your head high. You look satisfied with the event. You do not roll your eyes, drop your shoulders and exhale a great sigh. You are still on. You are being watched. And you sit down, stop or go back to your seat, walking tall and proud.

Chapter 10

PRACTISING AND PLANNING

"Practice is everything."
—Diogenes Laertius, Greek historian

Handling questions, like every other aspect of presentation requires practice, and finding the time to do so is up to you. This chapter is about practising. No coach can run the marathon or play the match for the athletes. Once you have the talk thought out and the points are on your cards, even if the visuals are not completed yet, it is time for you to start running through what you are going to say from beginning to end.

You practise your talk in part for timing, so put your watch on and start from the very beginning of the talk including your "Good morning" or "Good afternoon". Do not read it silently in your mind. Say it out loud, grope for the missing word, use your examples, tell your stories, take pauses and, as you do, think about where your visuals will be and start building in the pauses when you know that the audience will be looking at those visuals. If you recite the talk only in your head without the pause for the answer to the rhetorical question, or for the laugh, or for the overhead, your timing will be inaccurate. All those little additions take time. As you are saying the words aloud, you will also be discovering what words should be emphasised. You may want actually to underline them on the cards or draw two parallel lines between them to indicate a pause after a key question.

You may also discover that as you hear what you are saying, you decide that some data needs to be added, clarified or deleted. You may feel that you have too many arguments supporting your point, or that one of your arguments is too weak to be included, or that something that recently occurred in the office might be a good example to fit in. You may discover that you need transitions to move you from one point to the next.

Practising takes time, and you need to plan for it. By now you will have realised that presentation involves both a process and a product. Practising is part of the process that refines the product, the speech itself. If you are using note cards, carry them with you, and whenever you have a few minutes, take them out of your pocket or briefcase and work through them; that way you increase your comfort level with your own notes.

The Room

Now it is time for you to take a look at the room itself. When you asked the question, "where?" in your preparation, you were probably given a description of the venue. Now it is time to walk around the room to see it, to get a feel for its idiosyncrasies. In effect, you are on reconnaissance, you enter with all your antenna, absorbing information. What are the acoustics like? Are there heavy drapes and carpets? Will your voice be absorbed by them? Speak out loud. Will your voice be heard in the back or will you need to use a mike, and, if so, when will you have an opportunity to work with it?

What about the furniture? Are there tables and chairs? Are there only chairs there now, and do you need tables? Who provides them? When? What are the seats like? Straight backed, hard seats or deeply cushioned—the easier to relax in, or nod out in? How is the room arranged? Are the chairs in fixed positions or can they be moved? Do you want the room in theatre style or classroom style, or would you prefer a U shape? The advantage of the latter is that there are fewer barriers coming between you and the audience. The audience, too, can eyeball each other, not stare at the back of a neighbour's head.

What is at the front of the room for you? Is there a table, a lectern, a dais? Are they movable? Will there be a head table? How big is it? Can you move around it with ease? Will it be covered by a cloth, or are your legs and feet clearly visible to the audience? How high will the table or lectern be? Can you be seen over it? Remember the pictures of Queen Elizabeth in Washington DC, a few years ago? Only her head and hat appeared over the lectern. Someone had forgotten to check the facilities before she started her speech.

What are the sight lines? In other words, when you are
standing in the front of the room, if there were people in
every seat could you be seen from every angle? Is there a
pillar or a piece of equipment that blocks your view and
theirs? Do you need to move chairs back or prevent
people from sitting in certain seats? If you are using an
overhead, at what angle are you blocked by it? If you are
using a flip chart, where does it need to be placed for you
to write comfortably and for the audience to see? Whether
you are left handed or right handed will also determine
where to position it. Are there enough pads for the flip
chart? Pens or markers, pointers, erasers, chalk? Where
are the light switches? How dark is the room with or without lights? Can people take notes? Are there flexes across
the floor? Could you trip? Where are the power points?
Do you need additional leads?

Does the equipment work? Where are the power buttons? The volume control? The remote controls? Which
button controls what? Is there someone other than yourself
who could press some buttons? Is there room at the
speaker's table for your acetates and a glass of water? Is
where you are walking carpeted or will every footfall
echo? Therefore, should you change your choice of shoes?

Are there windows? Is the room drafty? What is visible
outside? Will people be walking by or is there heavy truck
traffic? How public are you? Can the windows be opened
or shut? How warm is the room when doors are closed?
Warm enough for people to become sleepy? Are there any
telephones? Will they ring? Can they be disconnected? Are
there speakers that will make the room sound like an airport or hospital? Can you control them? Are there doors
that people in an outside corridor can inadvertently open?

Details. Details. Details. Sound like a lot of work? It
isn't really, perhaps 10 or 15 minutes worth. That is what

you are looking for when you go into the room. You are checking for possible problems, and you are checking to increase your own comfort level with it just the way a dog or cat does before snuggling down into his or her corner. Make the room your own and get comfortable with it.

The Introductions

When you do your preparing, it is not all about the equipment, tables and chairs. There are human elements as well. Will you be introducing yourself or will someone else be introducing you? If it is someone else, what do you want them to say or not say about you or your talk? Sometimes an introduction by another person can take a good line from your talk or misstate the intent of your talk, so chat with him or her in advance. Where will that person be sitting? Where will you be sitting in relation to that individual? What is the person's name? Can you pronounce it? Will that person lead any post-talk questions, or will you? Do you want to? Will they or you make concluding remarks?

If you are beginning to wonder if there are rules about all this, if one way is better than another, or whether one method is right and another is wrong, the answer is "No." It is right, if you have thought through the implications of your decision, and you are comfortable that it is the appropriate approach. And if you are wondering why you should bother? Looking poised and at ease is more impressive than rushing into a room saying "Where do I speak from?" or "When do I start?" Your audience will not know when you have done your homework; they will know when you have not. There are enough spontaneous events that may occur during your talk, so why clutter your mind on the day with extraneous details like locating switches that could have been found in advance in just a few minutes?

Team Presentations

There is another aspect to your practising and planning that needs to be addressed and that relates to your being a member of a team presentation. There is no difference in your planning except that you will have asked the questions together or shared the answers so that you all have a clear sense of your brief. If you are working in a team, you will also need to divide the labour, to decide who is speaking on what, to compare notes on the data that each of you may be using and on the approach that each of you is taking.

A team presentation is not a team presentation just because three or four people happen to be talking. It involves team work in its truest sense. The unique talents of the members of the Irish soccer team are not brought together on the afternoon of a match without an opportunity for the players to practise together in advance. When speaking, you need to get used to each other's presentation styles, strengths, weaknesses and how best to use or diffuse them. You need to determine if, in terms of content, there is too much or too little overlap or none at all. Unless you talk among yourselves, one of you may make assumptions that the other person is handling some aspect that, in fact, is not being handled at all.

As a team, you also need to plan your own introductions. Will one of you be explaining who is going to say what, i.e., "Sean will address the long range plans, while I will be describing the current ones." Or will each of you introduce yourselves? How will you hand off the baton from one to the next? You also need to plan the question period. Which one of you will be taking which questions? Will one of you take all of the questions, or will you divide them up, depending on the focus? And if you are hit with a tough one, what's the support system?

You will also need to decide about the seating arrangements. Will each of you walk up from the audience or table? During the questions will you all be standing? And how will you refer to each other; "My colleague, Liam" or "Liam". When you pass the baton will you be "handing over" to Liam, or will you have a sentence that reintroduces Liam's section, for example, "Liam, will now discuss the reasons for _____" or "Liam is better able to _____".

Know that in a team presentation everyone, not just the speaker at the moment, is being watched. It is remarkable how often in team presentations, the team members look as though they have no use for each other. They look stone-faced. They do not listen when the other members speak. You should create the impression that you like each other, that you work together, and that you care about each other. You do that by looking interested in what the other person is saying, by listening and reacting to your own colleagues' words. If there is a joke, smile at it. If one of you makes a mistake, the other one should be ready to pick up.

In other words, practising is about controlling your environment to free you from unnecessary additional anxieties. You need to build in the time to run through your own talk, to refine and time it as well as going into the venue. Once there you need to examine the layout and the equipment carefully. If there are others involved, you need to talk with or work with them to ensure that the presentation runs smoothly.

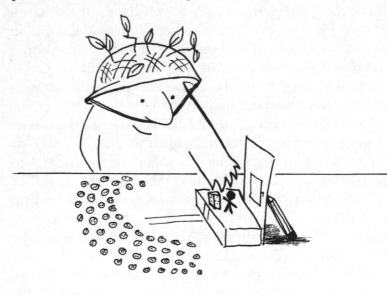

Chapter 11

HANDLING YOUR NERVES

"You have no reason to fear the wind if your
hay-bales are tied down."
—Irish proverb

"Considering how dangerous everything is,
nothing is really very frightening."
—Gertrude Stein

Now that the time for your presentation is nearing, you
are probably experiencing some doubts. This chapter is
devoted to your worries and offers some thoughts about
handling them. First of all, understand that you will always
be nervous before you talk. Stage fright is normal. A little
adrenaline energises the team, the athlete, the dancer or
the speaker. There is no reason to be ashamed or embar-
rassed. For most people nervousness does not last long
into the performance; it fades quickly. However, to understand better your own "fight or flight" response, it is helpful
once again to become more self-aware. In other words,
learn to recognise your own reactions when you are under
stress and then accept or compensate for them. By doing
so you can also diminish them.

The best cure for nerves, if there is one, is to do your
homework so that you are prepared. The better you know
the material, the audience, the venue, the less anxious you
will be. Running through your material in the room in

advance also increases your comfort level. In addition, rather than berating yourself for feeling nervous, remember that everyone gets nervous, not just you. We are all affected by the jitters in different ways. If you ask, you will discover that some people find that their palms or underarms are drenched with sweat. Some begin to feel their hearts pounding in their chests. Remember the expression, "my heart was in my mouth"? Others have a "hollow feeling" in the pit of their stomachs. Still others feel heat around their faces, and their necks are flushed. Still others feel the strength ebb from their legs, their hands tremble; in others, throats go dry. Some go to the loo more often. Do you recognise any of these symptoms? If you do, you have also probably noticed that the sensations ease as you gain control of your body and of the situation early in your talk.

Please note that this chapter is called "Handling your Nerves", not "Curing your Nerves". It is important to accept the fact that some nervousness is normal; however, there are some techniques that may ease the symptoms or at least help you to compensate for them.

For example, many people find that having a cup of tea or coffee before giving a talk helps them to focus their minds. It may. It may also heighten their anxiety. Eliminating coffee is one of the first suggestions for people who fear flying. Coffee is also a diuretic, so you may find yourself going off to the loo one more time. Consider, therefore, foregoing that last cup or two. That is particularly true if you have a sensitive stomach. Instead you might have some room-temperature water near where you are speaking. It is even more important if you know that your mouth tends to go dry. By the way, taking a sip is also a great excuse for a well-timed pause. If your legs do not quite feel as if they will hold you up, be sure that you know the route that takes you from where you are sitting to where you are speaking. Practise walking the path, especially if there are any steps that you might have to climb or descend. If there is a banister, hold on to it.

It is natural to worry that the audience will notice your trembling hands. Do not be concerned. They won't. When your hands are at their worst, the audience are looking at the warm expression on your face and are focused on your opening remarks. However, if you do not want to draw attention to your shaking hands, be sure that you have your first acetate already placed on the overhead projector before turning on the switch. You do not want the shadow of a trembling hand magnified and filling the screen for all of the audience to see.

Suppose your fear, though, is that you are going to panic and forget everything you planned to say. Although

we talked in Chapter 7 about using notes, it is important to mention their use here. The day that I went blank in front of the camera, I had *no* notes. I learned a lesson. Use notes. Consider writing down your opening sentences word for word on one card. If you have worked yourself into a state of panic, as I had, the precise words will be written down for you to know why you are speaking and what the subject is. As you ease into the next few sentences, the anxiety will be fading.

Remember that it is when you first begin your talk that you are most anxious; therefore, you may want to take the attention off yourself by creating a diversion, by designing an opening that moves the focus from you to something else. For example, you might ask the audience to talk briefly to each other about something you have planned, or you might have a visual projected on the screen or have a question pre-flipped. By doing that you will involve the audience in the activity or have them looking at something other than at you and your hands.

There are other techniques as well. It is important to remember that *you* are knocking the stuffing out of yourself with your self-doubts. First of all, remember the answer to "why me?" "Because we know you can do it", "You know more about the topic than anyone else", etc. Then, to ease stress of any kind, find the time to make a list of your accomplishments and keep it handy. Refer to it in advance of any stressful situation. You may say that you do not have any achievements, but you do. Realistic ones. Getting your leaving cert. or your driver's licence, going to another country and getting a job on your own, winning a particular match, finishing a certain project. We are not looking for lists that start off with "Winning the Nobel Prize". Just list things that you are proud of and that made you feel good.

In advance of the speech look at the list to remind yourself that you are a winner. What you are doing is replacing negative thoughts with positive ones. Also, consider taking a moment or two to go off on your own to calm yourself down. Close your eyes and visualise a tranquil place or moment that you have experienced. It may be a deserted beach, or a quiet forest scene or the water of a lake gently lapping against the shore. By closing your eyes and concentrating on that peaceful scene, you will relax.

In addition, take some good deep breaths and release them slowly. That is a particularly good idea when you are just about to speak. It is also one of the reasons why you need to stand tall with your chest up. Good posture enhances your ability to fill your lungs. Not only does it improve your voice but those deep breaths rather than shallow ones can calm you. So, do not begin to talk until you are ready and you have taken a good deep breath.

Treat nerves the way you do stress of any kind, so the recommendations are the same, including finding a few minutes to stretch your legs. Rather than pace in the hall or in your office, take a brisk 10-minute walk.

Suppose you are still making yourself crazy. Take one of your self-doubts and follow it to its natural conclusion. In other words, if you hear, "I will be desperate!" in your own mind, focus on it and start analysing it by asking yourself questions. "Well, now, what will be terrible? Why? *Then* what will happen to me if it is? And then what?" Force your mind to address the thought and take it to its logical conclusion. If you do, you will see that the outcomes are unrealistic. You are not going to die, be ostracised, exiled, imprisoned or made redundant. In essence, try to ease the stress with positive physical and mental activity.

Chapter 12

IT'S SHOW TIME

"The ability to speak is a short cut to distinction. It puts a man in the limelight, raises him head and shoulders above the crowd, and the man who can speak acceptably is usually given credit for an ability out of all proportion to what he really possesses."
—Lowell Thomas, American journalist

You have done your planning. You have asked your questions, you have written the material, you are looking good: shoes shining, hair trimmed, notes in hand, visuals in order, thoughts positive. It's show time! But no; you are not quite finished yet. There is more to do; remember the decisions you make are before, during and after.

Suppose your talk is part of a lengthier discussion, or you are one of a series of speakers. Then, on the day, you should be listening to what the others are speaking about before it is your turn. You do that to be able to modify your own speech based on what you have heard someone else say. For example, you may find that you disagree with another speaker, or agree with or like a particular phrase that was used, or realise that they have said something you have planned to say, so use it: "As Brendan said earlier ____" or "As Siobhan said, I must disagree that ____." "There is no need for me to explain what Malcolm stated so clearly but ____". Besides looking professional, you are role-modelling good listening skills for your audience.

In addition, on the day of your talk be aware of any noteworthy events that are currently in the news. There may be a major match, a sports trade, a literary award, a national election or 100 mile per hour winds. You might be able to incorporate one of the events into your talk as an analogy or example. Doing that may bring your message home once again or bring it to life.

By now, you have done all the planning and anticipating that you can do. It is now time to think on your feet, to handle whatever happens spontaneously as it occurs, to make instant decisions. Some you may anticipate, but others you will not. Let's suppose you have been introduced. You have begun—the audience is with you, all is well, but you make a mistake. You lose your train of thought, you misuse a word, you drop one of your note cards. Do not try to hide it. It happened. The audience may welcome the fact that you are being human and, as humans, we are fallible, so make the mistake and make it big. Smile, laugh, apologise. Collect your thoughts, find the right word or bend down and pick up the card. If you are quick-witted you may be able to incorporate some aspect of the error into your talk. Then let it go. It has happened, and it is over. Like a mishit in tennis. You mishit the ball. Now there is another point to play. If you dwell on the error, there may be another mishit. What does every sports announcer say? "____ has lost concentration." Regain yours.

Now suppose you are well into your talk, and two people enter the room late. Make an assessment. If you see members of the audience turning to look or to comment or acknowledge that person or persons, remember that at that moment you are not being listened to, so stop. Look pleasant. No point looking annoyed. Why make the newcomers feel more uncomfortable than they probably already are? Diffuse their discomfort with a smile. You are looking for friends, not enemies. Once they are settled, continue. Depending on how many or who, you may want to make a one or two sentence recap or indicate that "we were making the point that _____".

Well, you have had your error and your interruption. Do you think that now you can go on some sort of automatic pilot? No! Remember what was said about eye contact: looking and seeing what is happening? You need to be using the antenna again, this time to take in the smiles, the frowns, the glazed eyes, the doodling or note-taking, the side conversations. Because if you sense that the audience is beginning to fatigue or to lose interest, you know that you need to make a change.

Based on your knowledge of your own repertoire of talents, decide to do something different from what you are doing. This shift of tempo is like a symphony, with each movement written in another tempo. Maybe it is time to walk or to move more quickly. Maybe you have not played with your voice at all, so it is time to change the volume, take it down to a whisper or raise it. Do you think what you have been saying is too complicated or abstract? When did you notice that the audience started to fade? Is it time for a quick recap or for an example or anecdote? Should you have a window opened? Should you take a break? Should you eliminate an entire upcoming section that you had planned to discuss? Should you take questions? In other words, based on what is happening at the moment, you need to make a decision, to react, to do something different. What you choose to do is entirely up to you. By watching and gauging reactions and by making changes you will keep the presentation lively and energised. With your audience uppermost in your thoughts, you will be reacting to them and keeping them with you.

You have done it! Bask in the applause, pat yourself on the back. Sure, be relieved, but enjoy and be proud of what you have done. The audience will let you know that you did a good job. They will not know all the work that you put into preparation, but with the effort has come success. Like any professional, you made it look easy. When the presentation is over, you will be tired, possibly drained. Maintaining that degree of concentration during a talk is fatiguing. But while the event is still reasonably fresh in your mind, replay your own mental tape of the proceedings. Do not be hypercritical or start to nitpick—oh, I put my hand in my pocket four times, I said "em" too often, I looked at one side of the room too much. OK, you did. Pat yourself on the back for the things you did right, and

know that old habits will give way to new and better ones, so look at the big picture. Did the opening work? Were your arguments clear? Did the questions suggest that the audience understood your message?

Get some feedback from others; do not just rely on your own self-assessment. Find out what people liked and what worked. Listen to what people recall. Was it what you wanted them to remember? All of this data is added to your growing wealth of information, of ideas, techniques or approaches that seem to work for you or that may not. Learn from what you did to apply it to the next talk. Experiment.

In addition to your own self-assessment and feedback from friends, colleagues, and attendees, start observing other people. Look at people. Watch other speakers. Look at the way successful business men and women dress, look at their hair, the colour combinations, the fit of their clothes, their choice of jewellery. Look at TV, watch the news, go to the movies. Every time you do, every time you sit in a meeting, watch the speaker, watch the movement, the speech pattern, the facial expressions, the use of the hands, how mistakes are handled, how questions are handled, what visuals are used, what new technology. Ask yourself if it worked. Watch and listen to the audience. Develop a critical eye about what appears to be effective and what is not. Start saving stories or anecdotes for further reference. Most of all, look for excuses to speak again. Every time you stand up and speak you will be developing your skills. At the end of the day, presenting should be seen as an opportunity for you as an individual to shine and therefore for your organisation to shine as well.

Being able to give a good presentation is a marketable skill in today's competitive business environment. A person who can prepare and deliver an effective talk is an asset to any organisation. Someone who can sell, motivate, persuade, tell, encourage and/or entertain others is invaluable, because such people can win new business, encourage their staff, explain ideas clearly, articulate problems, present alternatives and justify decisions. When they do, people listen.

You can be such a person. Understand the principles and practise the skills. You may still say to yourself, "I'll be OK", "I'll be fine", "it will be over soon", no longer as a passive, dependent individual filled with anxiety, but rather from a position of knowledge and strength. The emphasis changes too because now, you *will* be OK, you *will* be fine and yes, it *will* be over soon. Undoubtedly there will be another day, another talk, another opportunity, because people will listen to you.